D1568159

Colossal Cookies

100 OUTRAGEOUSLY OVERSIZED TREATS THAT CHANGE THE BAKING GAME

Wendy Kou

CREATOR OF MY DESSERT DIET

PAGE STREET
PUBLISHING CO.

PAGE STREET
PUBLISHING CO.

First published in 2018 by
Page Street Publishing Co.
27 Congress Street, Suite 105
Salem, MA 01970
www.pagestreetpublishing.com

Distributed by Macmillan, sales in Canada by The Canadian Manda Group.

22   21   20   19   18   1   2   3   4   5

ISBN-13: 978-1-62414-672-5
ISBN-10: 1-62414-672-4

Library of Congress Control Number: 2018938284

Cover and book design by Rosie Stewart for Page Street Publishing Co.
Photography by Toni Zernik
Food styling by Scott Wiese

Printed and bound in China

Table of Contents

The Story of the Colossal Cookie

I LOVE cookies. Really . . . it's not just a casual, "I love cookies" statement, but a bold, standing-proud-on-the-roof-of-my-Brooklyn-apartment-waving-my-arms-in-the-air-declaring-to-the-world "I LOVE COOKIES!!" statement.

So, the colossal cookie came about when I decided that I wanted to be a little funny one day. I have my husband to thank for this, who has also reaped the benefits from my love for baking, and of course, cookies, and he reminded me that I was "trying to be on a diet." Well, diets don't work so well for me because I absolutely love sweets, so hence my blog My Dessert Diet. One Sunday morning I was baking cookies and made a bet with my husband that I would have just one cookie. He quickly agreed, without thinking twice, and then I was off making two cookies. Not just any kind of cookie, but in fact, one colossal cookie for myself and one regular-sized cookie for him. HA. The joke was on him.

After the two cookies came out of the oven, he quickly ran over to keep me honest to the bet, but then found out that I had decided to bake one massive, colossal cookie for myself that was bigger than my head and weighed more than three pounds. HA! So of course I won, but that was the sweet moment that the colossal cookie was born.

From there on out, I got more creative and started to stuff them, which really made it that much better. Nearly all the cookies in this book are stuffed with another cookie or filling, which creates that fun element of surprise that I just love and cannot get enough of. One of my favorite parts is breaking open the cookies to see the beautiful layer of stuffing inside.

In this book, I have compiled the best of the best colossal cookie recipes. I invite you to bake, and most importantly, to share colossal cookies with your friends and families. I've seen so many happy faces and mouths wide open with delight that I want you to share this fun and joy with everyone you know! Last, but not least, definitely have the time of your life, because I had the most fabulous time of my life creating this just for you.

Getting Started

The majority of the cookies in this book are stuffed, and to the right is a visual step-by-step of the process.

STUFFING THE COLOSSAL COOKIE

1. Start with two cookie dough balls; one for the top of the cookie and one for the bottom.

2. Use the palms of your hands to flatten the cookie dough balls to round circles (about ⅜ inch [1 cm] thick).

3. Add stuffing to the center of one of the flattened dough circles.

4. Place the other flattened dough over the stuffing.

5. Pinch the top and bottom edges of the cookie together and smooth out the sides for a seamless cookie, which creates a seal for the stuffing. This step is extremely important. If the sides open up while baking, the stuffing ingredients such as caramel, chocolate ganache or marshmallow will leak out from the sides. The cookie will be a dome-shape, but it will flatten out while baking.

6. Cover the entire cookie with chocolate chips or sprinkles and gently press them into the cookie dough to set them in place.

BAKING COLOSSAL COOKIES

All the recipes instruct you to place the cookies in the freezer anywhere from 15 to 30 minutes, but usually for at least 20 minutes. That time in the freezer allows the dough to chill and the flour and butter to rest, letting more of that amazing cookie flavor come out. If you're baking the cookies on the same day you make the dough, there is no need to cover or wrap the cookies, but if you would like to save the cookies to bake another time, wrap them individually in plastic wrap or aluminum foil. They can be kept in the refrigerator or freezer for up to two weeks. When ready to bake, be sure to place the cookie in the center of the baking sheet as it will spread out while baking. There is no need to thaw out the cookies before baking.

IS THE COLOSSAL COOKIE FULLY BAKED?

Because not all ovens are created equal, if the bake time is up and the center of the cookie appears to be raw, then leave it in the oven for another 3 to 5 minutes and continue to check until the center has a light crisp layer on top.

SHARING IS CARING

The size of each colossal cookie varies among the different recipes, but on average it will be 6 to 8 inches (15 to 20 cm) in diameter. If you're willing to share, one cookie can be shared by 2 to 4 people. The recipes all yield at least 2 cookies, which is perfect for 4 to 8 people. Also, the recipes can be doubled to make more colossal cookies so you can have more to yourself!

EXTRA COOKIE DOUGH

Some recipes may yield extra cookie dough. For any extra cookie dough, either keep it in plastic wrap and save it in the refrigerator or freezer for another time, or make traditional-sized cookies and bake at 350°F (177°C) for 12 to 15 minutes.

For more helpful tips to create fantastic colossal cookies, refer to the Techniques and Tips chapter (page 184).

Start with two cookie dough balls; one for the top of the cookie and one for the bottom.

Use the palms of your hands to flatten the cookie dough balls to round circles (about ⅜ inch [1 cm] thick). Add stuffing to the center of one of the flattened dough circles.

Pinch the top and bottom edges of the cookie together and smooth out the sides for a seamless cookie, which creates a seal for the stuffing. This step is extremely important. If the sides open up while baking, the stuffing ingredients will leak out from the sides.

Cover the entire cookie with chocolate chips or sprinkles and gently press them into the cookie dough to set them in place.

All-Time Favorites

My all-time favorite cookie recipes feature a variety of my go-tos and top 10 must-haves. It was quite a struggle to narrow it down to 10, but I promise that these are definite crowd pleasers, and there is something for everyone. I've tested these with friends, relatives, friends-of-friends and colleagues, and even the most stubborn dieter will make sure that their cheat-day falls on the day that you're making these cookies. AND, if you're looking to win that baking contest or show off at a school or work function, trust me, I've got the right recipes here for you!

But, just to make sure we're all on the same page, these are not only out-of-this-world amazing cookie recipes, they prove the saying "bigger is better." Without further ado, I would like to invite you to break out of the habit of making regular-sized cookies and start making these extraordinary, delicious, gooey and fun-to-break-apart colossal cookies.

Extra Chocolatey Chip + Marshmallow

Have you ever stood in a store so indecisive that you just could not decide between a chocolate chip or double chocolate chip cookie? You know for sure you don't want to get both—there's simply no need for the extra calories, but one part of your brain is whispering chocolate chip and the other part is screaming double chocolate chip. This cookie is one of my all-time favorites because I love having the best of both worlds!

Yield: 2 colossal cookies

CHOCOLATE CHIP COOKIE

¾ cup (103 g) bread flour

¼ cup (34 g) cake flour

½ tsp baking powder

½ tsp baking soda

¼ tsp salt

½ cup (114 g) unsalted butter

½ cup (110 g) packed dark brown sugar

½ cup (100 g) white granulated sugar

1 large egg, at room temperature

1 tsp pure vanilla ewtract

½ cup (85 g) chocolate chips

EXTRA CHOCOLATEY CHIP COOKIE

1 cup (125 g) all-purpose flour

⅔ cup (57 g) unsweetened cocoa powder

1 tsp baking powder

¼ tsp salt

½ cup (114 g) unsalted butter, at room temperature

¼ cup (51 g) shortening, at room temperature

½ cup (110 g) packed dark brown sugar

½ cup (100 g) white granulated sugar

1 large egg, at room temperature

1 tsp pure vanilla extract

2 tbsp (30 ml) heavy cream

½ cup (85 g) chocolate chips

ADDITIONAL INGREDIENTS

⅔ cup (30 g) mini marshmallows

⅔ cup (113 g) chocolate chips

For the chocolate chip cookie, whisk together the bread and cake flour, baking powder, baking soda and salt and set aside.

Use the paddle attachment on a stand mixer to cream together the butter and brown and white sugar on medium speed. Once the texture is fluffy and the color is light, reduce the speed to low and add in the egg. Once the egg is fully incorporated, add the vanilla.

With the mixer speed on low, add the flour mixture and continue mixing until the cookie dough just comes together. Add in the chocolate chips and continue mixing until the chocolate chips are evenly distributed in the dough.

For the extra chocolatey chip cookie, sift together the flour, cocoa, baking powder and salt to remove any cocoa powder clumps. Whisk together to ensure it is mixed well and set aside.

With the paddle attachment on a stand mixer, cream together the butter, shortening and brown and white sugar on medium speed until light and fluffy. Reduce the mixer to low speed and add in the egg. Once the egg is fully incorporated, add the vanilla, then the cream.

With the mixer on low speed, slowly add in the flour mixture. Once the cookie dough just comes together, pour in the chocolate chips and allow the mixer to continue for a few more seconds. If the dough feels too sticky, place it in the refrigerator for 5 to 10 minutes before working with it.

To assemble the cookies, line a jelly roll pan with parchment paper and use this as your work surface. Take ½ cup (120 g) of chocolate chip cookie dough and roll it into a round ball and set it on the parchment paper. Take ½ cup (120 g) of extra chocolatey chip cookie dough and roll it into a round ball. Take the 2 cookie dough balls and press and roll them together to create one cookie dough ball, but be sure to keep the chocolate chip on one side and the extra chocolatey chip on the other. Use the palms of your hands to flatten the cookie dough into a circle 5 inches (13 cm) in diameter. Be sure that the seams of the chocolate chip and extra chocolatey chip are down the middle of the area you flatten, so you have equal halves of both cookies.

Repeat the above steps to create a second flattened cookie circle. Take ⅓ cup (15 g) of mini marshmallows and place them in the center of one of the cookie circles, and then place the other flattened cookie dough on top. Use your fingers to pinch together the top and bottom edges of the cookie, and then smooth out the edges for a seamless finish. Repeat the above steps for the second cookie.

Spread the chocolate chips all over the top of the 2 cookies. Once both cookies are completed, place the cookies in the freezer and allow them rest for at least 20 minutes. Preheat the oven for 350°F (177°C).

Bake one cookie at a time for 26 to 30 minutes, or until the sides of the cookie are golden-brown. Allow the cookie to cool down on the baking tray for about 20 minutes before moving to prevent breakage.

Espresso Double Chocolate Chip

After baking my first colossal chocolate chip cookie, I wanted to expand and play with different combinations, so this recipe was my very first stuffed cookie. The outer chocolate chip layer is a little crispy and chewy, with a contrasting moist chocolate layer on the inside. Definitely have a little fun and interchange the two cookies—make one with chocolate chip as the outer layer and the other with the chocolate layer on the outside. Then you have two different cookies with one recipe!

Yield: 2 colossal cookies

CHOCOLATE CHIP COOKIE

1 cup plus 2 tbsp (154 g) cake flour

1 cup (137 g) bread flour

¾ tsp baking powder

¾ tsp baking soda

¾ tsp sea salt

½ cup plus 3 tbsp (156 g) unsalted butter, at room temperature

¾ cup plus 2 tbsp (193 g) packed dark brown sugar

½ cup (100 g) granulated white sugar

1 large egg, at room temperature

1 tsp pure vanilla extract

3 tbsp (45 ml) heavy cream

½ cup (85 g) chocolate chips

ESPRESSO DOUBLE CHOCOLATE CHIP COOKIE

1 cup (125 g) all-purpose flour

¼ cup (22 g) unsweetened cocoa powder

1 tsp espresso powder

½ tsp baking soda

⅛ tsp salt

½ cup plus 2 tbsp (142 g) unsalted butter, at room temperature

¾ cup (150 g) granulated white sugar

1 large egg, at room temperature

1 tsp pure vanilla extract

2 tbsp (30 ml) heavy cream

½ cup (85 g) chocolate chips

ADDITIONAL INGREDIENTS

⅔ cups (113 g) chocolate chips

For the chocolate chip cookie, whisk together the cake and bread flour, baking powder, baking soda and salt and set aside.

Use the paddle attachment on a stand mixer to cream together the butter and brown and white sugar on medium speed until the mixture is fluffy and light, about 2 to 3 minutes. Reduce the mixer speed to low and add in the egg. Once the egg is fully incorporated, add the vanilla, followed by the cream.

Keeping the mixer speed on low, add in the flour mixture. Mix until the cookie dough just comes together, and then add in the chocolate chips. Wrap the dough in plastic wrap to prevent it from drying out.

For the espresso double chocolate chip cookie, sift together the flour, cocoa, espresso powder, baking soda and salt. Whisk together to ensure all are well combined and set aside.

Use the paddle attachment on a stand mixer to cream together the butter and sugar on medium speed until it is light and fluffy, which will take about 3 to 4 minutes. Reduce the mixer speed to low and add in the egg. Once it is fully incorporated, add in the vanilla, followed by the cream.

Keeping the mixer speed on low, add in the flour mixture. Mix until the cookie dough just comes together. Add in the chocolate chips and continue to mix for a few more seconds.

To assemble the cookie dough, line a jelly roll pan with parchment paper and use this as your work area for the assembly.

Roll ⅔ cup (160 g) of the exterior cookie dough into a ball, and then flatten it with the palms of your hands to a circle 5 inches (13 cm) in diameter. Repeat this step so you have 2 flattened rounds of cookie dough.

For the inner layer, roll ⅓ cup (80 g) of the inner cookie dough into a ball, and then flatten it to a circle 3½ inches (9 cm) in diameter. Create 2 flattened rounds of cookie dough and place each of the smaller cookie rounds in the middle of the larger ones made in the previous step.

Assemble the cookie so that the 2 exterior cookies are surrounding the interior cookie. Use your fingers to pinch together the top and bottom edges of the cookie dough to create a seal and smooth out the sides for a seamless finish. Repeat the above steps for the second colossal cookie.

Cover the tops of both cookies with chocolate chips. Gently press the chocolate chips into the cookies to set them in place. The chocolate chips should cover the entire cookie top.

Place the cookies in the freezer for about 20 minutes. Preheat the oven to 350°F (177°C).

Bake one cookie at a time for 22 to 26 minutes, or until the edges are golden-brown. Once the cookie is removed from the oven, allow it to cool down on the baking sheet for at least 15 minutes before moving it to the cooling rack. If the cookie is moved too soon it can break easily.

Birthday Cake Cookie

The birthday cake cookie is great for any occasion, whether it actually is a celebration for a birthday, an engagement party, baby shower or just because. The best part about a colossal cookie is that most likely your friends and family haven't seen or had one yet. So impress everyone by having an out-of-this world cookie larger than everyone's head, and don't forget to take tons of photos so those memories can live on!

Yield: 3 colossal cookies

1½ cups (188 g) all-purpose flour

½ tsp baking powder

¼ tsp salt

½ cup (114 g) unsalted butter, at room temperature

1 cup (200 g) granulated white sugar

1 large egg, at room temperature

1 tsp pure vanilla extract

⅛ tsp almond extract

½ cup plus 3 tbsp (132 g) rainbow sprinkles, divided

Whisk together the flour, baking powder and salt and set aside.

Use the paddle attachment on a stand mixer to cream together the butter and sugar at medium speed until the mixture is fluffy and light, about 3 to 4 minutes. Reduce the mixer speed to low and then add in the egg. Allow the egg to become fully incorporated into the mixture before adding the vanilla and almond extract.

Keeping the mixer speed on low, add in the flour mixture. Mix until the cookie dough just comes together, and then add in ½ cup (96 g) of rainbow sprinkles. It's so much fun to watch the colorful sprinkles swirl into the dough!

Divide the cookie dough into 3 equal pieces. Roll each piece into a ball and flatten the balls into circles 5 inches (13 cm) in diameter. Place the cookies on a jelly roll pan and cover each cookie with 1 tablespoon (12 g) of sprinkles. Gently press the sprinkles into the cookies to set them in place. If you like, it's fun to add other types of sprinkles on top and mix in your favorite colors, but be aware that not all sprinkles are created equal and some may melt while baking.

Place the cookies in the freezer for at least 20 minutes to allow the dough to rest. Preheat the oven to 350°F (177°C).

Bake one cookie at a time for 18 to 22 minutes, or until the edges are light golden-brown. Once the cookie is removed from the oven, allow it to cool down on the baking tray for about 10 minutes. If the cookie is moved too soon it may break.

UNICORN BIRTHDAY CAKE VARIATION: Turn this colossal birthday cake cookie into a unicorn with a few simple steps! After you divide the dough into three parts, color one pink, one blue and one purple with gel food coloring. Mix until the desired color is reached and then continue with the recipe.

Chocolate-Hazelnut Spread Babka Cookie

The beauty of a Babka is its mesmerizing swirls and amazing layers of flavor created by blending sweetened bread with chocolate. For me, this cookie recipe is the absolute special treat for any get together to show off some skills—and it's really not hard to make. The chocolate-hazelnut spread is the ultimate finishing touch that will have everyone talking endlessly about this Babka cookie years later.

Yield: 2 colossal cookies

SUGAR COOKIE

¾ cup (103 g) bread flour

¾ cup (103 g) cake flour

1 tsp cream of tartar

1 tsp baking soda

¼ tsp salt

½ cup (114 g) unsalted butter, at room temperature

1 cup (200 g) granulated white sugar

1 large egg, at room temperature

1 tsp pure vanilla extract

2 tbsp (30 ml) heavy cream

CHOCOLATE COOKIE

1¼ cups (156 g) all-purpose flour

¾ cup (37 g) chocolate fudge instant pudding mix

¼ cup (22 g) unsweetened cocoa powder

1 tsp baking soda

¼ tsp salt

½ cup (114 g) unsalted butter, at room temperature

½ cup (100 g) granulated white sugar

½ cup (110 g) packed dark brown sugar

1 large egg, at room temperature

1 tsp pure vanilla extract

2 tbsp (30 ml) heavy cream

ADDITIONAL INGREDIENTS

½ cup (60 ml) chocolate-hazelnut spread (I prefer Nutella)

½ cup (85 g) mini chocolate chips

For the sugar cookie, whisk together the bread and cake flour, cream of tartar, baking soda and salt and set aside.

Use the paddle attachment on a stand mixer to cream together the butter and sugar on medium speed for 3 to 4 minutes until the mixture becomes light and fluffy. Reduce the mixer speed to low and add in the egg. Once the egg is fully incorporated, add in the vanilla, followed by the cream. Once the ingredients are well combined, add in the flour mixture. Stop the mixer after the dough just comes together. Wrap the cookie dough in plastic wrap to prevent it from drying.

For the chocolate cookie, sift together the flour, pudding mix, cocoa, baking soda and salt. Whisk to mix together thoroughly and set aside.

Use the paddle attachment on a stand mixer to cream together the butter and white and brown sugar on medium speed for 2 to 3 minutes until the mixture becomes fluffy and light. Reduce the mixer speed to low and add in the egg. Once the egg is fully incorporated, add the vanilla and the cream. After the mixture is smooth in texture, add in the flour mixture and mix until the cookie dough just comes together.

To assemble the Babka cookie, be sure to have a clean working area to roll out the cookie dough. Line a jelly roll pan with parchment paper and set to the side. Usually I sprinkle some flour or confectioners' sugar on the kitchen counter and roll the dough directly out on it, but because we do not want to add any more dry ingredients to the cookie dough, I recommend laying out a sheet of parchment paper over your work surface. Since parchment paper has a non-stick surface, it will make it easier for later steps.

With a rolling pin, roll out 1 cup (240 g) of sugar cookie dough into a 7½ by 11-inch (19 × 28-cm) rectangle less than ⅜ inch (1 cm) thick. On a separate work surface area, roll out ⅔ cup (160 g) of chocolate cookie dough into a 6½ by 10-inch (17 × 25-cm) rectangle. Lay the chocolate cookie dough in the center of the sugar cookie dough rectangle, leaving a border of sugar cookie dough around the edges. Don't worry if it breaks apart, just piece the chocolate cookie together on the sugar cookie. Use an offset spatula or knife to spread the chocolate-hazelnut spread evenly on the chocolate cookie dough surface area.

(continued)

Lay out a sheet of parchment paper and roll out your sugar cookie dough.

Roll out ⅔ cup (160 g) of chocolate cookie dough and lay it in the center of the sugar cookie dough.

Gently peel up the edges on the long side of the sugar cookie dough and roll it slightly.

Use a serrated knife to gently cut the roll lengthwise into equal halves.

Chocolate-Hazelnut Spread Babka Cookie (Continued)

Now it is time to roll the cookie dough together! Gently peel up the edges on the long side of the sugar cookie dough and roll it tightly. Once done, you will have a nicely rolled cookie dough that resembles a Swiss roll. Use a serrated knife to gently cut the roll lengthwise into equal halves. Once opened up you will see the beautiful layers of sugar cookie, chocolate cookie and chocolate-hazelnut spread. Place the two halves next to each other vertically facing you and pinch the top ends together. Carefully, take one half-roll and cross it over the top of the other, creating a multi-twisted braid, but always keep the open layers facing upwards. Pinch together the bottom ends to join the dough in one connected piece. Take the entire roll and carefully turn it so it is horizontal. The last step is to curl the dough around itself, as though you're making a wreath with the cookie, while keeping the open layers facing upwards and connecting the ends of the dough to itself to hold the shape together. Use your hands to shape the cookie, so it is rounded. Repeat the same steps above for the second Babka cookie.

Sprinkle the mini chocolate chips on top of the cookies. Place the cookies in the freezer for at least 30 minutes for the dough to rest. Preheat the oven to 350°F (177°C).

Bake one cookie at a time for 28 to 32 minutes, or until the sugar cookie edge is a light golden-brown color. Allow the cookie to cool down on the baking sheet for about 20 minutes prior to moving it to the cooling rack.

Create a twisted braid, keeping the layers facing up.

Create a circle with the twisted braid, similar to a wreath. Finish with chocolate chips on top.

Cinnamon Roll Cookie

Cinnamon and sugar always reminds me of my suburban childhood days strolling around the mall and suddenly being hypnotized by the wafting cinnamon-sugar aroma. The sweet warm scent always draws me in, and all I want in that moment is the cinnamon-sugar roll with that amazing sugar glaze all over it!! I could not resist merging a piece of my childhood memory with my love for cookies. This cinnamon roll cookie is a combination of a sugar cookie and cinnamon sugar filling with a classic glaze on top.

Yield: 4 colossal cookies

CINNAMON COOKIE

2¼ cups (281 g) all-purpose flour

1 tsp baking powder

½ tsp salt

½ cup (114 g) unsalted butter, at room temperature

¼ cup (51 g) shortening, at room temperature

¾ cup (150 g) granulated white sugar

1 large egg, at room temperature

1 tsp pure vanilla extract

3 tbsp (45 ml) heavy cream

FILLING

½ cup (114 g) unsalted butter, melted

⅔ cup (147 g) packed dark brown sugar

2 tsp (5 g) ground cinnamon

For the cookie dough, whisk together the flour, baking powder and salt and set aside.

Use a paddle attachment on a stand mixer to cream together the butter, shortening and sugar on medium speed. In 2 to 3 minutes, the texture will become fluffy and light. Reduce the mixer speed to low and add in the egg. Once the egg is fully incorporated into the batter, add in the vanilla, followed by the cream.

Keeping the mixer speed on low, add in the flour mixture and continue to mix until the cookie dough just comes together. Use a spatula to scrape the sides as needed, to help ensure the flour mixture and butter mixture come together.

For the cinnamon sugar filling, melt the butter in the microwave in a heatproof bowl. Mix the sugar and cinnamon with the melted butter.

To assemble the cookies, line a jelly roll pan with parchment paper and lay out a sheet of parchment paper over the work surface. Since parchment paper has a non-stick surface, it will make it easier for later steps.

Using a rolling pin (a wine bottle will work as well!), roll out one-quarter of the cookie dough to a rectangle about 12 inches long by 3½ inches wide (30 × 9 cm). Use a knife to cut the dough lengthwise into 3 long strips that are 1 inch wide (3 cm). Remove the excess dough around the strips, but do not peel the strips off the parchment paper just yet.

Use an offset spatula or silicone spatula to spread a layer of cinnamon sugar filling over the cookie dough strips.

Start from one end of the strips and gently roll up one strip. Once you have rolled one strip of dough, connect the end of that roll to the beginning of another strip by pinching and smoothing the dough together. Then, continue to roll the second strip onto the cinnamon roll, making an even larger cinnamon roll. Repeat again, so in the end, you've rolled together 3 long strips of cookie dough to create one large cookie cinnamon roll! In the end, each cinnamon roll will be around 4 inches (10 cm) in diameter.

(continued)

Use a rolling pin to roll out the cookie dough.

Use a knife to cut the dough lengthwise into 3 strips.

Spread a layer of cinnamon sugar filling over the strips.

Start from one of the ends and gently roll the strip of cookie dough.

Cinnamon Roll Cookie (Continued)

ICING

2 tbsp (28 g) unsalted butter, melted

1 cup (120 g) sifted powdered sugar

½ tsp pure vanilla extract

Move the completed cinnamon roll to the prepared tray and make 3 more cinnamon roll cookies. Place the tray in the freezer for at least 20 to 30 minutes for the dough to rest and preheat the oven to 350°F (177°C).

Make the icing while the cinnamon cookies are resting in the freezer. Place the butter in a heatproof bowl and microwave until the butter is melted. Whisk the melted butter with the sugar and vanilla until the mixture comes together. Since the sugar can be a powdery mess while mixing, I recommend first mixing ½ cup (60 g) of the sugar with the butter. After the first half is incorporated, add in the remainder along with the vanilla.

Bake 2 cinnamon rolls at a time, but be sure to place them on opposite ends of the baking sheet at least 3 inches (8 cm) from the edge, as they will spread while baking. Bake for 20 to 24 minutes, or until the edges are golden-brown. Allow the cookies to cool down on the baking tray for about 15 minutes after they are out of the oven, as they are fragile. Transfer to a cooling rack and drizzle the desired amount of icing over the cinnamon rolls!

Connect the first strip to the next strip and continue to roll the cookie dough.

Repeat the previous step one more time for a full cinnamon roll.

Red Velvet Cookie Stuffed with Cheesecake

I've always loved a great cheesecake, and what better way to enjoy a piece of cheesecake than to have it inside a colossal red velvet cookie! The combination of the velvety cookie plus the soft and airy cheesecake is what makes this cookie so fantastic. One bite and you'll instantly feel like you're in heaven, daydreaming about dancing around with red velvet cookies while fluffy cheesecake clouds float above you. One of the best parts about this recipe is that there will be some leftover cheesecake to indulge in while you're waiting for your cookies to bake!

Yield: 3 colossal cookies

1½ cups (188 g) all-purpose flour

¼ cup (22 g) unsweetened cocoa powder

½ tsp baking soda

½ tsp baking powder

¼ tsp salt

½ cup plus 2 tbsp (142 g) unsalted butter, at room temperature

½ cup (110 g) packed light brown sugar

½ cup (100 g) granulated white sugar

1 large egg, at room temperature

1 tsp pure vanilla extract

2 tbsp (30 ml) heavy cream

2 tbsp (30 ml) red food coloring or gel coloring

3 (3-inch [3.5-cm]) squares Cheesecake (page 179), or store-bought

¾ cups (128 g) white chocolate chips

For the red velvet cookie, sift together the flour, cocoa, baking soda, baking powder and salt. Whisk together to ensure that all parts are well combined and set aside.

Use the paddle attachment on a stand mixer to cream together the butter and brown and white sugar on medium speed. After about 2 to 3 minutes, the texture of the mixture will become fluffy and light in color. Reduce the mixer speed to low and add in the egg, followed by the vanilla and cream, adding each ingredient after the previous is fully mixed in. Add in the red gel food coloring. I prefer gel food coloring, because there is less liquid, and it does not affect the batter as much, but either way the cookies will be absolutely delicious.

Add the flour mixture and mix until the cookie dough comes together. If the dough feels too sticky to work with, place it in the refrigerator for 10 to 15 minutes.

To assemble the cookies, line a jelly roll pan with parchment paper and use this as your work area.

Divide the dough evenly into 3 parts, about 1 cup (240 g) each. Divide each piece in half again, for the tops and bottoms of the cookies.

Roll each piece of dough into a ball, and then use the palms of your hands to flatten the balls into circles 4½ inches (11 cm) in diameter. Place one cheesecake square in the middle of each of the cookie dough circles. Place the other flattened cookie dough circles over the cheesecake. Use your fingers to pinch together the top and bottom edges of the cookie dough, and then smooth out the sides to create a seamless finish to the colossal cookie.

Gently press the white chocolate chips all over the top of each cookie. Normally, I do incorporate some chocolate chips into the cookie batter, but with the red velvet cookie and cheesecake, the white chocolate chips are only needed on top for the perfect balance, adding a slight bit of sweetness to each bite.

Place the tray of cookies in the freezer for at least 20 minutes for the cookie dough to rest. Preheat the oven to 350°F (177°C).

Bake one cookie at a time for 22 to 26 minutes. Once the cookie is removed from the oven, allow it to cool down on the baking sheet for about 15 minutes. If the cookie is moved too soon to the cooling rack, it could break apart easily.

RED VELVET STUFFED WITH BROWNIE VARIATION: If you love brownies, then definitely make the red velvet cookie recipe and stuff it with a brownie. Make the Chocolate Brownie recipe (page 180) and substitute 3-inch (7.5-cm) brownie squares for the cheesecake. Once the stuffed red velvet cookie is ready to be baked, follow the same instructions for baking and cooling.

Browned Butter Cornflake S'mores

Summer is my favorite season for many reasons—warm and sunny weather, beach time, BBQs—but most importantly . . . s'mores! I love the combination of the toasted and gooey marshmallow with warm and melted chocolate all inside a crispy graham cracker shell. In the s'mores version of a cookie, I wanted to have a little more crisp, so I found the right balance by adding cornflake cereal. The cookie flavor is enhanced with the nutty aroma from the brown butter. Stuffed with chocolate ganache, plus marshmallows on top—it's the best s'mores cookie ever!

Yield: 2 colossal cookies

1 cup (125 g) all-purpose flour

½ tsp baking powder

¼ tsp salt

½ cup (120 ml) unsalted Browned Butter (page 183)

½ cup (110 g) packed light brown sugar

½ cup (100 g) granulated white sugar

1 large egg, at room temperature

1 tsp pure vanilla extract

1 cup (45 g) mini marshmallows, divided

¾ cup (128 g) chocolate chips, divided

⅓ cup plus ¼ cup (61 g) coarsely crushed graham crackers, divided

1 cup (30 g) cornflake cereal, divided

6 tbsp (90 ml) Dark Chocolate Ganache (page 178), or store bought

For the s'mores cookie, whisk together the flour, baking powder and salt and set aside.

Use a stand mixer with a paddle attachment on medium speed to mix the browned butter and brown and white sugar. Since the sugar will be wet from the butter, the mixture may stick to the sides of the mixing bowl. If that happens, scrape the sides before moving to the next steps.

Reduce the mixer speed to low and add in the egg. Once the egg is fully incorporated, add the vanilla. Once the egg and vanilla are added, the mixture will become more smooth and easy to mix. When the liquid ingredients are fully incorporated, add in the flour mixture.

Once the cookie dough just comes together, add in ⅔ cup (30 g) of mini-marshmallows and ½ cup (85 g) of chocolate chips and continue to mix for a few more seconds. Add in ⅓ cup (35 g) of crushed graham crackers and ¾ cup (23 g) of cornflakes. Mix only enough to incorporate; otherwise the graham crackers and cornflakes will be crushed to crumbs.

To assemble the cookies, line a jelly roll pan with parchment paper and use this as your work area.

Divide the cookie dough into 4 equal pieces. Roll each piece of dough into a ball, and then use the palms of your hands to flatten the balls into circles 5 inches (13 cm) in diameter.

Spoon 3 tablespoons (45 ml) of chocolate ganache onto the centers of 2 of the flattened cookie dough circles. Top with the other dough circles and use your fingers to pinch together the top and bottom edges. Smooth out the sides for a seamless colossal cookie.

Add the finishing touches by covering the top of the cookie with the remaining chocolate chips, marshmallows, cornflakes and graham crackers. Gently press each of the toppings into the cookie to set it in place.

Place the tray with the cookies in the freezer for at least 20 minutes for the dough to rest. Preheat the oven to 350°F (177°C).

Bake one cookie at a time for 22 to 26 minutes, or until the edges are golden-brown. Once the cookie is removed from the oven, allow it to cool on the baking sheet for 20 minutes prior to moving it to the cooling rack, otherwise, it may break apart easily.

Peanut Butter Jelly Cookie

My cookie version of a classic PB & J always brings back memories of the good old days. The cookie is stuffed with a layer of peanut butter and jelly, similar to the classic sandwich, but what makes this even better is the outer layer is a peanut butter cookie! The combination of the slightly crisp peanut butter cookie layer with the gooey peanut butter and jelly on the inside makes this simply irresistible.

Yield: 2 colossal cookies

1 cup (240 g) peanut butter, divided

½ cup (69 g) bread flour

¾ cup (103 g) cake flour

½ tsp baking powder

½ tsp baking soda

¼ tsp salt

½ cup (114 g) unsalted butter, at room temperature

½ cup plus 2 tbsp (138 g) packed dark brown sugar

¼ cup plus 2 tbsp (76 g) granulated white sugar

1 large egg, at room temperature

½ tsp pure vanilla extract

½ cup (120 ml) favorite jelly

Prep the peanut butter stuffing. Line a jelly roll pan with parchment paper. Spread ¼ cup (60 g) of peanut butter on the parchment paper to create a circle about 4 inches (10 cm) in diameter. Repeat. Place the pan with the peanut butter in the freezer. Freezing the discs of peanut butter will make it easier for the peanut butter to sit on top of the jelly.

For the peanut butter cookie, whisk together the bread and cake flour, baking powder, baking soda and salt and set aside.

Use the paddle attachment on a stand mixer to cream together the butter with the brown and white sugar on medium speed for about 2 to 3 minutes until light and fluffy. Reduce the mixer speed to low, and then add ½ cup (120 g) of peanut butter. Allow it to fully mix together before proceeding.

Keeping the mixer speed on low, add in the egg. Once the egg is fully incorporated, add the vanilla. Once the ingredients are combined, add in the flour mixture and mix until the cookie dough just comes together.

To assemble the cookies, line a jelly roll pan with parchment paper and use this as your work area for the assembly.

Remove the peanut butter discs from the freezer and place to the side. The peanut butter should be solid and pliable, making it easy to remove from the parchment paper, but if the peanut butter is still sticky, place the peanut butter back in the freezer for another 5 to 10 minutes

Divide the cookie dough into 4 equal pieces. Roll each piece into a ball, and then use the palms of your hands to flatten the balls into circles 5 inches (13 cm) in diameter.

Spread ¼ cup (60 ml) of jelly onto the centers of 2 of the flattened circles. It may be easier to use a tablespoon to scoop the jam onto the cookie, since this would allow you to control the placement and spread of the jam. If you're using this method, use 4 tablespoon-size scoops of jam, which is equivalent to ¼ cup (60 ml).

Peel the peanut butter discs from the parchment paper, and place them on top of the jelly. Top with the other flattened cookie dough circles. Use your fingers to pinch together the top and bottom edges of the cookie circles to create a seal and smooth out the sides to create a seamless colossal cookie.

For finishing touches, use chopsticks or skewers to imprint a criss-cross design on top of the cookie. Place the completed cookies in the freezer for at least 20 minutes for the cookie dough to rest. Preheat the oven to 375°F (191°C).

Bake one cookie at a time for 18 to 22 minutes, or until the edges are golden-brown. Once the cookie is removed from the oven, allow the cookie to cool down on the baking sheet for about 15 minutes before moving to a cooling rack. The cookie is fragile while hot and can break apart easily.

Billionaire Cookies

The Billionaire Cookie originated as a millionaire bar that I took to the next level. This bar is one of my favorite items to bring to a potluck party, knowing that it will be the hit of the night. I knew that I had to incorporate the millionaire bar somehow in cookie form, so I've adapted the original concept of a bar layered with a chocolate chip cookie base, chocolate ganache, shortbread and caramel to create my Billionaire Cookie. Trust me, when I say that this recipe is out-of-this-world, it really is! I will sneak into the kitchen at night just to have another bite of this cookie before I go to bed.

Yield: 2 colossal cookies

CHOCOLATE CHIP COOKIE

1 cup (137 g) bread flour

1 cup (137 g) cake flour

½ tsp baking powder

½ tsp baking soda

½ tsp cornstarch

½ tsp salt

½ cup (114 g) unsalted butter, at room temperature

2 tbsp (26 g) shortening

½ cup (110 g) packed dark brown sugar

½ cup (100 g) white granulated sugar

1 large egg, at room temperature

1 tsp pure vanilla extract

3 tbsp (45 ml) heavy cream

CHOCOLATE COOKIE

1 cup (125 g) all-purpose flour

⅓ cup plus 1 tbsp (34 g) unsweetened cocoa powder

1 tsp baking soda

1 tsp cornstarch

½ tsp salt

½ cup (114 g) unsalted butter, at room temperature

½ cup (110 g) packed dark brown sugar

½ cup (100 g) granulated white sugar

1 large egg, at room temperature

1 tsp pure vanilla extract

For the chocolate chip cookie, whisk together the bread and cake flour, baking powder, baking soda, cornstarch and salt and set aside.

Use the paddle attachment on a stand mixer to cream together the butter, shortening and brown and white sugar at medium speed. After 2 to 3 minutes, the mixture will become fluffy and light in color. Reduce the mixer speed to low and add in the egg. Once the egg is fully incorporated, add in the vanilla and cream.

Keeping the mixer speed on low, add the flour mixture. Stop the mixer once the cookie dough just comes together. Wrap the cookie dough in plastic wrap to prevent it from drying out. On a side note, the chocolate chip cookie dough may appear to be missing an obvious ingredient—chocolate chips! Don't worry, we'll be adding them to the cookie at the very end.

For the chocolate cookie, sift together the flour, cocoa, baking soda, cornstarch and salt. Whisk to ensure all the ingredients are well combined and set aside.

Use the paddle attachment on a stand mixer to cream together the butter and brown and white sugar on medium speed for 2 to 3 minutes. Reduce the mixer speed to low and add in the egg. Once the egg is fully incorporated, add in the vanilla.

With the mixer speed on low, add in the flour mixture and continue to mix until the cookie dough just comes together. Feel free to stop the mixer and scrape the sides as needed to ensure that the flour mixture is fully incorporated into the dough. Wrap the dough in plastic wrap to prevent it from drying out.

(continued)

Billionaire Cookies (Continued)

SHORTBREAD

⅔ cup (83 g) all-purpose flour

¼ tsp salt

½ cup (114 g) unsalted butter, at room temperature

⅓ cup (67 g) sugar

1 tsp pure vanilla extract

ADDITIONAL INGREDIENTS

6 tbsp (90 ml) Salted Caramel (page 177), or store-bought

⅔ cup (113 g) chocolate chips

Last, but not least, for the shortbread, whisk together the flour and salt and set aside.

Use the paddle attachment on a stand mixer to cream together the butter and sugar on medium speed for about 3 to 4 minutes. Once the mixture is light and fluffy, reduce the mixer speed to low and add in the vanilla extract.

With the mixer speed on low, add in the flour mixture and continue until the cookie dough just comes together.

To assemble the cookies, line a jelly roll pan with parchment paper and use this as your work area.

Roll ½ cup (120 g) of chocolate chip cookie dough into a ball, and then use the palms of your hands to flatten it into a circle 4½ inches (11 cm) in diameter. Roll ¼ cup (60 g) of chocolate cookie dough into a ball, and flatten it into a circle 3 inches (8 cm) in diameter. Place the chocolate cookie dough in the center of the flattened chocolate chip cookie dough. Roll ¼ cup (60 g) of shortbread into a ball, and then flatten it into a circle 3 inches (8 cm) in diameter and place on top of the chocolate cookie dough.

Use your fingers to create a concave area in the shortbread to hold the salted caramel. Scoop 3 tablespoons (45 ml) of salted caramel into the concave area of the shortbread. Roll another ½ cup (120 g) of chocolate chip cookie dough into a ball, and flatten it to a circle 4½ inches (11 cm) in diameter. Gently place the chocolate chip cookie dough over the layers of cookie dough and salted caramel. Use your fingers to pinch together the top and bottom edges of the chocolate chip cookie dough, and then smooth out the sides to create a seamless cookie. It is extremely important that the chocolate chip cookie dough is thoroughly sealed or the caramel could leak out through the seams while baking.

Use ⅓ cup (57 g) of chocolate chips to thoroughly cover the top of the cookie and set them in place by gently pressing them into the cookie dough.

Repeat the above steps for the second colossal cookie. Once the cookies are completed, place the tray in the freezer for at least 30 minutes for the cookie dough to rest before baking. Preheat the oven to 350°F (177°C).

Bake one cookie at a time for 28 to 32 minutes, or until the edges are golden-brown and the center of the cookie dough has a light crisp layer to it. Allow the cookie to cool down for about 20 minutes on the baking tray prior to moving to the cooling rack. These cookies are extremely delicate right out of the oven, especially with the melted caramel on the inside. Sometimes the salted caramel may come through on the top of the cookie, giving you a tease of what you have to look forward to!

Double Chocolate Chip + Birthday Cake Cookie

Sprinkle lovers beware . . . this could be your new favorite cookie! A chocolate cookie that is completely covered with sprinkles, plus stuffed with a birthday cake sugar cookie! While this cookie could sound like sprinkle overload, the soft double chocolate chip cookie creates a nice balance with the birthday cake sugar cookie. This cookie is perfect for the ice cream sundae lover who daydreams about chocolate and vanilla ice cream covered with sprinkles!

Yield: 2 colossal cookies

DOUBLE CHOCOLATE CHIP COOKIE

1 cup (125 g) all-purpose flour

¼ cup (22 g) unsweetened cocoa powder

½ tsp baking soda

⅛ tsp salt

½ cup plus 2 tbsp (142 g) unsalted butter, at room temperature

¾ cup (150 g) granulated white sugar

1 large egg, at room temperature

1 tsp pure vanilla extract

2 tbsp (30 ml) heavy cream

½ cup (85 g) chocolate chips

BIRTHDAY CAKE SUGAR COOKIE

1 cup (125 g) all-purpose flour

½ tsp baking soda

¼ tsp salt

½ cup (114 g) unsalted butter, at room temperature

1 cup (100 g) granulated white sugar

1 large egg, at room temperature

1 tsp pure vanilla extract

¼ tsp almond extract

½ cup (96 g) rainbow sprinkles

ADDITIONAL INGREDIENTS

⅔ cup (128 g) rainbow sprinkles

For the double chocolate chip cookie, sift together the flour, cocoa, baking soda and salt. Whisk to ensure all the ingredients are well combined and set aside.

Use the paddle attachment on a stand mixer to cream together the butter and sugar on medium speed for about 2 to 3 minutes until fluffy and light. Reduce the mixer speed to low and add in the egg. Once the egg is fully incorporated, add the vanilla, followed by the cream.

With the mixer speed on low, add in the flour mixture and continue to mix until the cookie dough just comes together. Add in the chocolate chips. Wrap the dough in plastic wrap to prevent it from drying out.

For the birthday cake sugar cookie, whisk together the flour, baking soda and salt and set aside.

Use the paddle attachment on a stand mixer to cream together the butter and sugar on medium speed. After 3 to 4 minutes, the mixture will become fluffy and light. Reduce the mixer speed to low and add in the egg. Once the egg is fully incorporated add the vanilla and almond extract.

Keep the mixer speed on low and add in the flour mixture. Once the cookie dough just comes together, add in the rainbow sprinkles. I love watching the rainbow of sprinkles swirl into the creamy white cookie dough! After a few seconds, the sprinkles should appear to be evenly distributed. Stop the mixer and it's time to assemble the cookie!

To assemble the cookies, line a jelly roll pan with parchment paper and use this as your work area for the assembly.

Divide the double chocolate chip cookie dough into 4 equal pieces. Roll each piece of dough into a ball, and then flatten the balls into circles 5 inches (13 cm) in diameter.

(continued)

Double Chocolate Chip +
Birthday Cake Cookie (Continued)

Take ⅓ cup (80 g) of birthday cake sugar cookie dough and roll it into a ball, and flatten it into a circle 3½ inches (9 cm) in diameter. Place the birthday cake sugar cookie dough in the center of one of the flattened double chocolate chip cookie circles. Take the other double chocolate chip cookie dough and place it over the birthday cake sugar cookie. Use your fingers to pinch together the top and bottom edges of the double chocolate chip cookie circles, and then smooth out the edges for a seamless finish. Repeat for the second colossal cookie.

Use ⅓ cup (64 g) of sprinkles to cover the surface area of each chocolate cookie. If you feel that you need more sprinkles to cover the cookie, definitely do so! When the cookie is baking, it will spread out, so though the sprinkles may appear to be clumped together, it will be perfect once baked.

Place the tray with the cookies in the freezer for the cookie dough to rest for at least 20 minutes. Preheat the oven to 350°F (177°C).

Bake one cookie at a time for 24 to 28 minutes. If you're unsure if the cookie is fully done, check to see if the edges are a little cracked, because that's one sign that it's ready! Once the cookie is removed from the oven, allow it to cool down on the baking tray for about 10 to 15 minutes prior to moving to the cooling rack to prevent breakage.

BIRTHDAY CAKE SUGAR COOKIE WITH CHOCOLATE SURPRISE VARIATION:

Have some extra fun by creating the inverse of the cookie with the birthday cake sugar cookie on the outside and the chocolate cookie on the inside with a layer of chocolate ganache for a fun surprise.

For the chocolate ganache, either make your own from the recipe on page 178 or buy a jar from the store. To incorporate the ganache, after the flattened chocolate cookie dough is placed in the center of the flattened birthday cake cookie, scoop 2 tablespoons (30 ml) of ganache on top of the chocolate cookie. Place the other flattened birthday cake cookie dough on top and use your fingers to pinch together the top and bottom edges, and then smooth out the sides to create a seamless finish. Be sure that the edges are well sealed, otherwise the ganache could leak out while baking. Follow the same baking and cooling instructions.

Chocolate Chip!

I absolutely love a classic chocolate chip cookie, and therefore, it really needs its own chapter in this book. The classic chocolate chip cookie is probably the most popular cookie. We commonly see chocolate chip cookies in stores and at restaurants, and we often bake them at home. Though the core ingredients are fairly simple, there are so many ways to make this classic cookie. And that is why I needed to present to you this chapter filled with deliciousness! Each cookie has its own twist that makes it unique and that will draw you back to this chapter time and time again.

Double Chocolate Chip + Sprinkles

A chocolate chip cookie stuffed with a double chocolate chip cookie and sprinkles and topped with more sprinkles . . . need I say more?

Yield: 2 colossal cookies

CHOCOLATE CHIP COOKIE

1 cup plus 2 tbsp (154 g) cake flour

1 cup (137 g) bread flour

¾ tsp baking powder

¾ tsp baking soda

¾ tsp sea salt

½ cup plus 3 tbsp (156 g) unsalted butter, at room temperature

¾ cup plus 2 tbsp (193 g) packed dark brown sugar

½ cup (100 g) granulated white sugar

1 large egg, at room temperature

1 tsp pure vanilla extract

3 tbsp (45 ml) heavy cream

½ cup (85 g) chocolate chips

DOUBLE CHOCOLATE CHIP COOKIE

1 cup (125 g) all-purpose flour

⅓ cup (29 g) unsweetened cocoa powder

¼ tsp baking powder

¼ tsp baking soda

¼ tsp salt

½ cup (114 g) unsalted butter, at room temperature

¾ cup (150 g) granulated white sugar

1 large egg, at room temperature

1 tsp pure vanilla extract

½ cup (85 g) chocolate chips

ADDITIONAL INGREDIENTS

¾ cup (144 g) rainbow sprinkles

⅔ cups (113 g) chocolate chips

For the chocolate chip cookie dough, whisk together the cake and bread flour, baking powder, baking soda and salt and set aside.

Using the paddle attachment on a stand mixer, cream together the butter and brown and white sugar on medium speed for about 2 to 3 minutes, until the mixture is fluffy and light. Reduce the mixer speed to low and add in the egg. Once the egg is fully incorporated add the vanilla, followed by the cream. Once the liquid ingredients are fully combined, add in the flour mixture and continue to mix until the cookie dough just comes together. Add in the chocolate chips and mix until incorporated. Wrap the cookie dough in plastic wrap to prevent it from drying out.

For the double chocolate chip cookie, sift together the flour, cocoa, baking powder, baking soda and salt. Whisk together the ingredients and set aside.

Use the paddle attachment on a stand mixer to cream together the butter and sugar on medium speed for about 3 to 4 minutes until light and fluffy. Reduce the mixer speed to low and add in the egg. Once the egg is fully incorporated, add the vanilla. With the mixer speed on low, add in the flour mixture and continue to mix until the dough just comes together. Add the chocolate chips and mix until incorporated.

To assemble the cookies, line a jelly roll pan with parchment paper and use this as your work area. Roll ⅔ cup (160 g) of chocolate chip cookie dough into a ball. Use the palms of your hands to flatten the dough into a circle 5 inches (13 cm) in diameter. Repeat this step 3 more times. Roll ⅓ cup (80 g) of double chocolate chip cookie dough into a ball, and flatten it into a circle 3½ inches (9 cm) in diameter. Repeat 3 more times and place one double chocolate chip cookie circle on top of each chocolate chip cookie circle. You now have four chocolate chip cookies topped with double chocolate chip cookies.

Create a concave area within 2 of the double chocolate chip cookie circles by using your fingers to gently press into the dough—don't worry if the cookie dough spreads out a bit. Pour 2 tablespoons (24 g) of sprinkles into the concave area. Top with the other chocolate chip/double chocolate chip cookie circles and pinch together the top and bottom edges to create a seal. Smooth out the edges for a seamless cookie.

For the finishing touches, sprinkle ¼ cup (48 g) of rainbow sprinkles over each cookie. Gently press the sprinkles into the cookie to set them in place, and then add ⅓ cup (57 g) of chocolate chips. Completely cover the top of the cookie, since it will spread out while baking.

Place both cookies in the freezer for at least 30 minutes for the cookie dough to rest. Preheat the oven to 350°F (177°C). Bake one cookie at a time for 24 to 30 minutes, or until the edges are golden-brown. I recommend checking on the cookie at the 24-minute mark. Allow the cookie to cool down for at least 15 to 20 minutes before moving to a cooling rack to prevent breakage.

Combo Red Velvet Stuffed with Cheesecake

Do you love chocolate chips and red velvet? Why not have them both combined in one cookie? What about a classic cheesecake? It's not such a classic once it's stuffed into a chocolate chip and red velvet cookie. If you're a cheesecake lover such as myself, good luck mustering up the generosity to share this one!

Yield: 3 colossal cookies

CHOCOLATE CHIP COOKIE

1¼ cups (156 g) all-purpose flour

⅓ cup (46 g) bread flour

¾ tsp baking soda

¼ tsp salt

½ cup plus 2 tbsp (142 g) unsalted butter

¾ cup (165 g) packed dark brown sugar

¼ cup (50 g) granulated white sugar

1 large egg, at room temperature

1 tsp pure vanilla extract

½ cup (85 g) chocolate chips

RED VELVET COOKIE

1½ cups (188 g) all-purpose flour

¼ cup (22 g) unsweetened cocoa powder

½ tsp baking powder

½ tsp baking soda

¼ tsp salt

½ cup plus 2 tbsp (142 g) unsalted butter, at room temperature

½ cup (110 g) packed light brown sugar

½ cup (100 g) granulated white sugar

1 large egg, at room temperature

1 tsp pure vanilla extract

2 tbsp (30 ml) heavy cream

2 tbsp (30 ml) red food coloring or gel coloring

ADDITIONAL INGREDIENTS

3 (3-inch [8-cm]) squares Cheesecake (page 179), or store-bought

½ cup (85 g) dark chocolate chips

½ cup (85 g) white chocolate chips

For the chocolate chip cookie, whisk together the all-purpose and bread flour with the baking soda and salt and set aside.

Using the paddle attachment on a stand mixer, cream together the butter and brown and white sugar on medium speed until the mixture is pale and fluffy. Reduce the mixer speed to low and add in the egg. Once the egg is fully incorporated, add the vanilla.

With the mixer speed on low, add in the flour mixture and continue to mix until the cookie dough just comes together. Add in the chocolate chips and mix for a few more seconds. Wrap the cookie dough in plastic wrap to prevent it from drying out.

For the red velvet cookie, sift together the flour, cocoa, baking powder, baking soda and salt. Whisk to ensure that they are well combined and set aside.

Use the paddle attachment on a stand mixer to cream together the butter and brown and white sugar on medium speed for about 2 to 3 minutes. Reduce the mixer speed to low and add in the egg. Once the egg is fully incorporated, add the vanilla and cream. Add in the red coloring. I prefer gel food coloring because there is less liquid, and it does not affect the cookie dough as much.

After the liquid ingredients are combined, add in the flour mixture. Once the cookie dough comes together, set it aside. If the dough feels too sticky, place it in the refrigerator for 10 to 15 minutes prior to working with it.

To assemble the cookies, line a jelly roll pan with parchment paper and use this as your work area.

Roll ⅓ cup (80 g) of chocolate chip cookie dough into a ball. Roll ⅓ cup (80 g) of red velvet cookie dough into a ball. Press the 2 dough balls together to create one cookie dough ball, but keep the chocolate chip on one side and the red velvet on the other. Use the palms of your hands to flatten the cookie dough into a circle 5 inches (13 cm) in diameter, with the seam of the 2 cookies in the middle.

Repeat the above steps to create a total of 6 flattened cookie circles. Take one of the cheesecake squares and place it in the center of one of the flattened cookie circles, and then place another flattened cookie on top. Pinch together the top and bottom edges of the cookie, and then use your fingers to smooth out the sides for a seamless finish to the cookie. Repeat to form the other 2 cookies.

Gently press the dark chocolate chips on the chocolate chip cookie side and the white chocolate chips on the red velvet side. Feel free to take on some creative freedom and mix it up or randomly place the chocolate chips as you wish.

Place the tray of cookies in the freezer for at least 20 minutes for the cookie dough to rest. Preheat the oven to 350°F (177°C).

Bake one cookie at a time for 25 to 30 minutes, or until the edges are golden-brown. Once the cookie is removed from the oven, allow it to cool down on the baking sheet for about 20 minutes. If the cookie is moved too soon, it could break apart easily.

Fluffy Chocolate Chip

While almost all the recipes in this book are flat colossal cookies, this one doesn't spread out while it's baking like the others, but it's still colossal in size! By using cold ingredients when we typically use room temperature ingredients, this fluffy cookie keeps its shape with its melt-in-your-mouth layers. I love breaking open this colossal cookie and seeing all the glistening chocolate chips! Simply a beautiful sight and so incredibly soft!

Yield: 2 colossal cookies

1 cup (137 g) bread flour

¼ cup plus 2 tbsp (49 g) all-purpose flour

½ tsp baking powder

½ tsp baking soda

½ tsp cornstarch

¼ tsp salt

¼ cup (57 g) unsalted butter, cold and diced

¼ cup (51 g) shortening, cold

¼ cup (55 g) packed light brown sugar

2 tbsp (28 g) packed dark brown sugar

¼ cup (50 g) granulated white sugar

1 large egg, cold

1 tsp pure vanilla extract

½ cup plus ⅔ cup (198 g) chocolate chips, divided

Whisk together the bread and all-purpose flour, baking powder, baking soda, cornstarch and salt and set aside.

Using the paddle attachment on a stand mixer, cream together the butter and shortening with the light brown, dark brown and white sugar on medium speed for about 2 to 3 minutes, until the texture is fluffy and light in color. Unlike mixing ingredients at room temperature, there will be small bits of butter in the mixture, which is what creates the decadent texture in the fluffy cookies.

Reduce the mixer speed to low and add in the egg. Once the egg is fully incorporated, add the vanilla. When the liquid ingredients are well incorporated, add in the flour mixture. When the cookie dough just comes together, add in ½ cup (85 g) of chocolate chips and allow the mixer to continue for a few more seconds.

Line a jelly roll pan with parchment paper and use this as your work area for the assembly.

Measure 1⅓ cups (320 g) of cookie dough and roll it into a ball, and then use the palms of your hands to flatten it into a circle 4½ inches (11 cm) in diameter and about 1 inch (2.5 cm) thick. After it bakes, it will expand by an inch to 5½ inches (13 cm) in diameter and keep its leavened dome shape. Repeat the above step for the second cookie.

Cover the tops of the cookies with the remaining chocolate chips and gently press them into the cookie to set them in place. Place the cookies in the freezer for at least 20 to 30 minutes. Preheat the oven to 365°F (185°C).

If your baking sheet is large enough, you can bake both at one time, but I still prefer to bake one at a time in the center of the cookie sheet. Bake for 22 to 26 minutes, or until the edges are golden-brown. Allow the cookie to cool down on the baking tray for about 15 minutes prior to moving it to the cooling rack.

FLUFFY CHOCOLATE CHIP COOKIE ICE CREAM SANDWICH VARIATION

1 pint (473 g) ice cream

3 tbsp (45 ml) Salted Caramel (page 177), or store bought

3 tbsp (45 ml) Dark Chocolate Ganache (page 178), or store bought

¼ cup (43 g) mini chocolate chips

Follow the Fluffy Chocolate Chip Cookie recipe and allow the cookies to completely cool down.

Allow the ice cream to warm slightly. Scoop the entire pint into the mixing bowl on a stand mixer with paddle attachment. On the lowest speed, add in the caramel, ganache and chocolate chips and stir for a few seconds. Once the toppings appear to be evenly distributed, place the bowl in the freezer to re-freeze the ice cream for 15 to 20 minutes.

Scoop the ice cream mixture onto the bottom side of one chocolate chip cookie and then place the other cookie on top. If the ice cream appears too soft, place the sandwich back in the freezer for another 15 to 20 minutes, or until ready to be eaten. Don't wait too long or someone else might beat you to it!

Chocolate-Hazelnut Stuffed Cookie

The silky and luxurious texture of chocolate-hazelnut spread (aka Nutella) makes it the perfect complement for many snacks and sweets, and nothing could be better than stuffing it inside a classic chocolate chip cookie. But, wait, there's nothing classic about this chocolate chip cookie—the crispy and chewy bread flour cookie combined with mini and regular-sized chocolate chips makes this cookie all the more outrageous! I love using the mini chocolate chips to incorporate into the dough and using the regular-sized chocolate chips on the outside for a fun contrast, but definitely mix it up and see what combination you can come up with! And oh yeah, it's stuffed with Nutella—but I didn't have to say that twice now, did I?

Yield: 2 colossal cookies

¾ cup (103 g) bread flour

½ cup (69 g) cake flour

½ tsp baking powder

½ tsp baking soda

¼ tsp salt

½ cup (114 g) unsalted butter, at room temperature

3 tbsp (39 g) shortening, at room temperature

¾ cup (165 g) packed dark brown sugar

½ cup (100 g) granulated white sugar

1 large egg, at room temperature

1 tsp pure vanilla extract

¾ cup (128 g) mini chocolate chips

½ cup (120 g) chocolate-hazelnut spread (I prefer Nutella)

½ cup (85 g) chocolate chips

Whisk together the bread and cake flour, baking powder, baking soda and salt and set aside.

Use the paddle attachment on a stand mixer to cream together the butter, shortening and brown and white sugar. After about 2 to 3 minutes, the mixture will become pale and fluffy. Reduce the mixer speed to low and add in the egg. Once the egg is fully incorporated, add the vanilla.

With the mixer speed on low, add in the flour mixture and mix until the cookie dough just comes together. Add in the mini chocolate chips and mix for a few more seconds.

To assemble the cookies, line a jelly roll pan with parchment paper and use this as your work area.

Divide the cookie dough into 4 equal pieces. Roll each piece into a ball and flatten the balls into circles 5 inches (13 cm) in diameter.

Use your fingers to gently press into the centers of 2 flattened circles to create a concave area to hold the chocolate-hazelnut spread. Scoop ¼ cup (60 g) of spread onto each center. It's easier to use a spoon or tablespoon (4 tablespoons equals ¼ cup), than a cup to have more control over the placement of the spread onto the cookie.

Place the other flattened cookie dough on top and use your fingers to pinch together the top and bottom edges, and then smooth out the sides for a seamless colossal cookie.

For the finishing touches, top each cookie with ¼ cup (43 g) of regular-sized chocolate chips by gently pressing them all over into the cookie for them to set in place.

Place the tray of the cookies in the freezer to allow the dough to rest for at least 20 minutes. Preheat the oven to 350°F (177°C).

Bake one cookie at a time for 28 to 32 minutes, or until the edges are golden-brown. Allow the cookie to cool down on the baking tray for about 20 minutes before moving it to the cooling rack.

CHOCOLATE CHIP COOKIE STUFFED WITH MARSHMALLOW VARIATION:
Chocolate chips and marshmallows go beautifully hand-in-hand, so definitely try substituting marshmallows for the chocolate-hazelnut spread. Each cookie will need ⅓ cup (15 g) of mini marshmallows. Marshmallow fluff can also be used and will be just as delicious!

Marshmallow, Nuts + More Cookie

This cookie is a nut-lover's dream come true! The stuffing combination of mixed nuts and peanut butter enhances that sweet and nutty aroma that we all love so much. The vanilla pudding mix in this recipe keeps these cookies extra soft, so you can indulge for days on soft cookies with crunchy mixed nuts—though I'm not sure why any cookies would still be around after the first day! The chewy chocolate chip cookie, gooey marshmallow plus nuts creates a party cookie mix in your mouth!

Yield: 2 colossal cookies

1¼ cups (156 g) all-purpose flour

¼ cup (13 g) vanilla instant pudding mix

½ tsp baking soda

¼ tsp salt

7 tbsp (98 g) unsalted butter, at room temperature

2 tbsp (26) shortening, at room temperature

½ cup (110 g) packed light brown sugar

½ cup (100 g) granulated white sugar

1 large egg, at room temperature

½ tsp pure vanilla extract

1 cup (170 g) chocolate chips, divided

⅓ cup plus ½ cup (42 g) mini marshmallows, divided

⅓ cup plus ¼ cup (76 g) coarsely chopped mixed nuts, divided

⅔ cup (160 g) peanut butter

Whisk together the flour, pudding mix, baking soda and salt and set aside.

Use the paddle attachment on a stand mixer to cream together the butter and shortening with the brown and white sugar on medium speed. After 2 to 3 minutes, the mixture will become light and fluffy. Once achieved, reduce the mixer speed to low and add in the egg. Once the egg is fully incorporated, add the vanilla.

With the mixer speed on low, add in the flour mixture. Once the cookie dough just comes together, add in ½ cup (85 g) of chocolate chips, ⅓ cup (17 g) of marshmallows and ⅓ cup (43 g) of nuts, and continue to mix for a few more seconds.

To assemble the cookies, line a jelly roll pan with parchment paper and use this as your work area.

Roll ⅔ cup (160 g) of cookie dough into a ball, and then use the palms of your hands to flatten it into a circle 5 inches (13 cm) in diameter. Repeat the above step 3 more times.

Scoop ⅓ cup (80 g) of peanut butter onto the centers of 2 of the cookie circles. Spread the peanut butter into a circle about 3 inches (8 cm) in diameter. Take the other flattened cookie circle and place it on top of the peanut butter. Pinch together the top and bottom edges of the cookie and smooth out the sides to create a seamless cookie.

Place both cookies on the parchment paper and divide the remaining chocolate chips, marshmallows and nuts between the cookies and gently press in place on top. Place the cookies in the freezer for at least 20 minutes for the dough to rest. Preheat the oven to 350°F (177°C).

Bake one cookie at a time for 22 to 26 minutes, or until the edges are golden-brown. Once the cookie is removed from the oven, allow it to cool down on the baking tray for about 10 to 15 minutes. If it is moved too soon, it can break apart easily.

Candy Bar Cookie

I had the biggest sweet tooth growing up and had secret candy stashes just for myself. So, for all those times I refused to share, here I am, sharing a chocolate chip cookie covered with candy bars. The candy bars on top of this cookie may appear to be decorative, but those yummy candy bar flavor notes will naturally mix with the cookie dough while baking. You'll be so happy to indulge in soft candy bar chunks, slightly crisp chocolate chip cookie and a soft chocolate ganache center.

Yield: 2 colossal cookies

⅔ cup (91 g) bread flour

½ cup (69 g) cake flour

½ tsp baking powder

½ tsp baking soda

¼ tsp salt

½ cup plus 2 tbsp (142 g) unsalted butter, at room temperature

½ cup (100 g) granulated white sugar

½ cup (110 g) packed dark brown sugar

1 large egg, at room temperature

1 tsp pure vanilla extract

½ cup (85 g) chocolate chips

7 tbsp (98 ml) Dark Chocolate Ganache (page 178), or store-bought

⅔ cup (112 g) chopped favorite candy bar(s)

⅔ cup (112 g) M&M's or Reese's Pieces

For the chocolate chip cookie, whisk together the bread and cake flour, baking powder, baking soda and salt and set aside.

Use the paddle attachment on a stand mixer to cream together the butter and white and brown sugar on medium speed for 2 to 3 minutes, until the mixture is pale in color and fluffy in texture. Reduce the mixer speed to low and add in the egg. Once the egg is fully incorporated, add the vanilla.

With the mixer speed on low, add in the flour mixture and continue to mix until the cookie dough just comes together. Add in the chocolate chips and mix for a few more seconds until they are evenly distributed.

To assemble the cookies, line a jelly roll pan with parchment paper and use this as your work area.

Divide the dough into 4 equal pieces. Roll each piece into a ball. Use the palms of your hands to flatten the balls into circles 4½ inches (11 cm) in diameter. Use your fingers to gently press into the center of 2 of the flattened halves to create a small concave area to hold the ganache. Scoop 3½ tablespoons (53 ml) of ganache onto the center of the concave area. Place the other flattened cookie circles over the chocolate ganache. Use your fingers to pinch together the top and bottom edges of the cookie, and then smooth out the sides to create a seamless finish.

Now, for the fun part! Arrange the chopped up pieces of your favorite candy bars all over the cookie. Gently press the candy bars onto the cookie dough to set them in place. Don't forget to add some bright colors to the cookie with M&M's or Reese's Pieces! After you're done decorating your cookies, place the tray in the freezer for the cookie dough to rest for at least 20 minutes. Preheat the oven to 350°F (177°C).

Bake one cookie at a time for 22 to 26 minutes, or until the edges are golden-brown. Once the cookie is out of the oven, allow it to cool down on the baking tray for 10 to 15 minutes. If moved too soon, it could break apart easily.

Peanut Butter + Chocolate-Hazelnut Striped Cookie

People tend to stare when they see colossal cookies—and while they're wondering if you're going to offer to share, you can break this cookie open, unveiling beautiful peanut butter and chocolate-hazelnut spread stripes. By then, even the shyest person would muster up the courage to ask you for even just the smallest piece. Now, the question for you is, will you share?

Yield: 2 colossal cookies

1 cup (137 g) bread flour

1 cup (137 g) cake flour

½ tsp baking powder

½ tsp baking soda

½ tsp cornstarch

½ tsp salt

½ cup (114 g) unsalted butter, at room temperature

2 tbsp (26 g) shortening, at room temperature

½ cup (110 g) packed dark brown sugar

½ cup (100 g) granulated white sugar

1 large egg, at room temperature

1 tsp pure vanilla extract

3 tbsp (45 ml) heavy cream

¼ cup (60 g) chocolate-hazelnut spread (I prefer Nutella)

¼ cup (60 g) peanut butter

⅔ cup (113 g) chocolate chips

Whisk together the bread and cake flour, baking powder, baking soda, cornstarch and salt and set aside.

Use the paddle attachment on a stand mixer to cream together the butter, shortening and brown and white sugar at medium speed. After 2 to 3 minutes, the mixture will become fluffy and light. Reduce the mixer speed to low and add the egg. Once the egg is fully incorporated, add the vanilla, followed by the cream.

With the mixer speed on low, add in the flour mixture. Stop the mixer once the cookie dough just comes together.

To assemble the cookies, line a jelly roll pan with parchment paper and use this as your work area.

Divide the cookie dough into 4 equal pieces. Roll each piece into a ball, and then use the palms of your hands to flatten the balls into circles 5 inches (13 cm) in diameter.

Leaving a 1-inch (2.5-cm) border of cookie dough, spread 1 tablespoon (15 g) of chocolate-hazelnut spread onto the top quarter of one circle, creating a small horizontal stripe. Spread 1 tablespoon (15 g) of peanut butter to make a stripe below the chocolate-hazelnut. Repeat to form 2 more stripes. Spread stripes on the second dough circle.

Gently cover the stripes with another cookie circle. Do not press in the center area of the cookie because you'll have peanut butter and chocolate-hazelnut spread oozing out from the sides. Use your fingers to pinch together the top and bottom edges of the cookie dough, and then smooth out the sides for a seamless finish.

For finishing touches, use ⅓ cup (57 g) of chocolate chips to cover the entire top of each cookie, and gently press the chocolate chips into the cookie to set them in place. Place the tray with the cookies in the freezer for the dough to rest for at least 20 minutes. Preheat the oven to 350°F (177°C).

Bake one cookie at a time for 24 to 28 minutes, or until the edges are golden brown and the center of the cookie has a light crisp layer on it. Allow the cookie to cool down on the baking tray for about 20 minutes prior to moving it to the cooling rack.

Brownie-Stuffed Cookie

The fluffy chocolate chip cookie combined with a decadent chocolate brownie makes this chocolate chip cookie unassuming from the outside and all the more special once you open it up and see the surprise on the inside!

Cold ingredients help the cookie keep its dome shape—so definitely make sure that the ingredients are cold. For good measure, I dice the butter and then place it in the freezer with the shortening for 5 to 10 minutes. If you use warm ingredients and the cookie spreads out with the brownie in the center, you'll end up with a cookie that looks like a flying saucer with a brownie dome in the center!

Yield: 4 colossal cookies

CHOCOLATE CHIP COOKIE

2 cups (274 g) bread flour

¾ cup (94 g) all-purpose flour

1 tsp baking powder

1 tsp baking soda

1 tsp cornstarch

½ tsp salt

½ cup (114 g) unsalted butter, cold and diced

½ cup (103 g) shortening, cold

½ cup (100 g) granulated white sugar

½ cup (110 g) packed light brown sugar

¼ cup (55 g) packed dark brown sugar

2 large eggs, cold

2 tsp (10 ml) pure vanilla extract

½ cup (85 g) chocolate chips

ADDITIONAL INGREDIENTS

4 (3-inch [8-cm]) pieces square Brownies (page 180)

1⅓ cups (227 g) chocolate chips

For the chocolate chip cookie, whisk together the bread and all-purpose flour, baking powder, baking soda, cornstarch and salt and set aside.

Using the paddle attachment on a stand mixer, cream together the butter and shortening with the white, light and dark brown sugar on medium speed until the mixture is fluffy and pale. When using cold butter, there will be small bits of butter in the mixture, which is what we want and adds that amazing texture in the fluffy cookies.

Reduce the mixer speed to low, add in the eggs one at a time, followed by the vanilla. Add in the flour mixture and continue to mix until the cookie dough just comes together. Add in the chocolate chips and allow the mixer to continue for a few more seconds for the chips to be evenly distributed in the dough.

To assemble the cookies, line a jelly roll pan with parchment paper and use this as your work area.

Divide the cookie dough into 4 equal parts, about 1⅓ cups (320 g) each. Divide each piece in half and roll it into a ball. Use the palms of your hands to flatten each ball into a circle 4 inches (10 cm) in diameter.

Place the brownies in the middle of the flattened cookie circles and top with the remaining circles. Pinch the top and bottom edges of the cookie dough together to create a seal, and then use your fingers to smooth out the sides for a seamless finish.

Cover each cookie with ⅓ cup (57 g) of chocolate chips and gently press them into the cookie dough. Place the tray with the cookies in the freezer for at least 20 to 30 minutes for the cookie dough to rest. Preheat oven to 350°F (177°C).

Bake one cookie at a time for 24 to 28 minutes, or until the edges are golden-brown. Once the cookie is out of the oven, allow it to cool down on the baking sheet for about 15 to 20 minutes before moving it to a cooling rack.

FLUFFY CHOCOLATE CHIP COOKIE STUFFED WITH CHEESECAKE VARIATION: Make the Cheesecake (page 179) recipe and cut it into quarters. Substitute the cheesecake for the brownies and follow the same instructions for baking and cooling.

Salted Caramel–Stuffed Cookie

I am obsessed with salted caramel! In the past, any time I saw the words "salted caramel" I bought as much as I could, until I realized that I should just learn how to make it myself. It is fairly simple to make, and it's always better when it's homemade. This combination of the sweet chocolate chips and the slight saltiness from the caramel is the perfect pairing to satisfy anyone's sweet cravings!

Yield: 2 colossal cookies

1¼ cups (156 g) all-purpose flour

⅓ cup (46 g) bread flour

¾ tsp baking soda

¼ tsp salt

½ cup plus 2 tbsp (142 g) unsalted butter

¾ cup (165 g) packed dark brown sugar

¼ cup (50 g) granulated white sugar

1 large egg, at room temperature

1 tsp pure vanilla extract

6 tbsp (90 ml) Salted Caramel (page 177), or store-bought

⅔ cup (113 g) chocolate chips

For the chocolate chip cookie, whisk together the all-purpose and bread flour, baking soda and salt and set aside.

With the paddle attachment on a stand mixer, cream the butter and brown and white sugar together on medium speed for 2 to 3 minutes, until light and fluffy. Reduce the mixer speed to low and add in the egg. Once the egg is fully incorporated, add the vanilla.

Add in the flour mixture and stop the mixer once the cookie dough comes together.

To assemble the cookies, line a jelly roll pan with parchment paper and use this as your work area.

Roll ⅔ cup (160 g) of cookie dough into a ball, then use the palms of your hands to flatten the dough into a circle 5 inches (13 cm) in diameter. Repeat 3 more times.

Use your fingers or a spoon to gently press into the center of 2 of the flattened cookie circles to create a concave area to hold the salted caramel. Place 3 tablespoons (45 ml) of salted caramel in the concave centers. Take the other flattened cookie circles and place them over the salted caramel. Be careful not to press onto the center of the cookie or some of the caramel may ooze out from the sides. Use your fingers to pinch the top and bottom edges together, and then smooth out the sides for a seamless finish.

Cover the tops of each cookie with ⅓ cup (57 g) of chocolate chips and gently press them in place. Place the cookies in the freezer for at least 30 minutes for the cookie dough to rest. Preheat the oven to 350°F (177°C).

Bake one cookie at a time for 22 to 26 minutes, or until the edges are golden-brown. Once the cookie is out of the oven, allow it to cool down on the baking tray for about 20 minutes before moving it to the cooling rack. When the cookie is hot, especially with the hot liquid caramel in the center, it can break apart easily.

Browned Butter Chocolate Chunk

The browned butter and toffee in this recipe result in a slightly crispier cookie with an amazing and unique nutty aroma. The creamy texture and natural flavors of the peanut butter round out the entire experience. This cookie's complexity is similar to a fine wine with layers of flavors, but doesn't require the years of aging.

Yield: 2 colossal cookies

½ cup (69 g) bread flour

½ cup (63 g) all-purpose flour

¼ cup plus 2 tbsp (52 g) cake flour

½ tsp baking powder

½ tsp baking soda

½ tsp salt

½ cup plus 2 tbsp (150 ml) unsalted Browned Butter (page 183)

½ cup (110 g) packed dark brown sugar

½ cup (100 g) granulated white sugar

1 large egg, at room temperature

1 tsp pure vanilla extract

1 cup (240 g) chocolate chunks, divided

⅓ cup + ¼ cup (140 g) Toffee (page 181) or store bought, divided

½ cup (120 g) peanut butter

For the chocolate chip cookie, whisk together the bread, all-purpose and cake flour, baking powder, baking soda and salt and set aside.

Using the paddle attachment on a stand mixer, mix the browned butter and brown and white sugar on medium speed. Since we are using melted browned butter, the sugar will be wet, which sometimes makes it harder to mix, so use a spatula to scrape the sides as needed. After the butter and sugar are mixed together, reduce the mixer speed to low and add in the egg. The mixture will become smoother when mixed with the egg. Once the egg is incorporated into the mixture, add the vanilla.

With the mixer speed on low, add in the flour mixture and continue to mix until the cookie dough just comes together. Add in ½ cup (60 g) of the chocolate chunks and ⅓ cup (80 g) of the toffee and mix it for a few more seconds.

To assemble the cookies, line a jelly roll pan with parchment paper and use this as your work area.

Roll ⅔ cup (160 g) of cookie dough into a ball, and then use the palms of your hands to flatten it into a circle 4½ inches (11 cm) in diameter. Repeat 3 more times.

Divide the peanut butter between 2 of the flattened cookie circles and spread it into a circle 3 inches (8 cm) in diameter. Place the other flattened cookie dough over the peanut butter. Use your fingers to pinch together the top and bottom edges of the cookie dough and gently smooth out the sides for a seamless cookie.

Decorate the cookies by gently pressing the remaining chocolate chunks and chopped toffee onto the tops of each cookie. Place the tray with the cookies in the freezer for the dough to rest for at least 20 minutes. Preheat the oven to 350°F (177°C).

Bake one cookie at a time for 22 to 26 minutes, or until the edges are golden-brown. Once the cookie is removed from the oven, let the cookie cool down on the baking tray for 15 minutes prior to moving it to the cooling rack. If the cookie is moved too soon, it could easily break apart.

Fluffy Chocolate Chip + Cookies 'n' Cream and Peanut Butter

So, imagine this . . . small crispy bits of Oreo cookie with peanut butter. Okay, that's already a pretty awesome combo. Next, stuff that combination into a chocolate chip cookie. But not just any chocolate chip cookie—a fluffy cookie that has soft layers that just break apart so easily. Just imagine it—and now go make it! You're welcome.

The fluffy cookie is a result of cold ingredients, so make sure the butter, shortening and egg are well chilled.

Yield: 2 colossal cookies

1 cup (137 g) bread flour

¼ cup plus 2 tbsp (49 g) all-purpose flour

½ tsp baking powder

½ tsp baking soda

½ tsp cornstarch

¼ tsp salt

¼ cup (57 g) unsalted butter, cold and diced

¼ cup (51 g) shortening, cold

¼ cup plus 2 tbsp (83 g) packed light brown sugar

¼ cup (50 g) granulated white sugar

1 large egg, cold

1 tsp pure vanilla extract

½ cup (120 g) peanut butter

1 cup (108 g) crushed Oreos, divided

⅔ cup (113 g) chocolate chips

For the chocolate chip cookie, whisk together the bread and all-purpose flour, baking powder, baking soda, cornstarch and salt and set aside.

Using the paddle attachment on a stand mixer, cream together the butter, shortening and brown and white sugar for about 2 to 3 minutes on medium speed until the texture is fluffy and light. There will be small bits of butter in the mixture, which is what adds the amazing texture in the fluffy cookies.

Reduce the mixer speed to low, and add in the egg. Once the egg is incorporated into the mixture, add the vanilla. Once the ingredients are incorporated together, add in the flour mixture and stop the mixer once the cookie dough just comes together.

To assemble the cookies, line a jelly roll pan with parchment paper and use this as your work area.

Roll ⅔ cup (160 g) of cookie dough into a ball, and then use the palms of your hands to flatten the dough into a circle 5 inches (13 cm) in diameter. Repeat 3 times.

Divide the peanut butter between 2 flattened cookie circles, and spread it into a circle 3 inches (8 cm) in diameter. On top of the peanut butter, add ¼ cup (27 g) of crushed Oreos for each cookie. Top with a flattened cookie circle and use your fingers to pinch together the top and bottom edges of the cookie and smooth out the sides for a seamless cookie.

Divide the chocolate chips and remaining Oreos and sprinkle all over the tops of each cookie and gently press to set in place. Place the tray with the cookies in the freezer for the cookie dough to set for at least 20 minutes. Preheat the oven to 365°F (185°C).

Bake one cookie at a time for 22 to 26 minutes, or until the edges are golden-brown. Once the cookies are removed from the oven, let them cool down on the baking tray for about 15 minutes prior to moving it to the cooling rack. If the cookie is moved too soon, it could easily break apart.

FLUFFY CHOCOLATE CHIP WITH PEANUT BUTTER + DARK CHOCOLATE GANACHE VARIATION: For the Dark Chocolate Ganache variation, either make the recipe on page 178 or use store-bought ganache. Follow the same instructions for the cookie dough. Stuff the cookie by scooping ¼ cup (60 g) of peanut butter onto the center of the cookie followed by ¼ cup (60 ml) of chocolate ganache on top of the peanut butter. Use the same baking and cooling instructions.

Chocolate Cravings

Do you ever have that insatiable urge for chocolate? You try to fend it off by distracting yourself with working or chores, or perhaps by eating a savory snack in the hope that it might do the trick? But it really doesn't. I've had those moments more than I would like to admit. These chocolate cookie recipes more than just satisfy my chocolate cravings, they make me jump for joy!

In this chapter, every chocolate cookie recipe is not just a chocolate cookie recipe—each one is stuffed with other elements that make it even better, such as more chocolate, marshmallow, dulce de leche and much, much more! That simple chocolate bar just can't compete.

Chocolatey, Chocolate Cookie

If you're having one of those days in which one piece of chocolate just isn't going to do it, well, I have just what you need. A soft chocolate cookie stuffed with gooey chocolate ganache and a mix of milk and dark chocolate chips—plus chocolate sprinkles on top! This is definitely not your everyday chocolate cookie.

Yield: 2 colossal cookies

1 cup (125 g) all-purpose flour

⅔ cup (57 g) unsweetened cocoa powder

1 tsp baking powder

¼ tsp salt

½ cup (114 g) unsalted butter, at room temperature

¼ cup (51 g) shortening, at room temperature

½ cup (100 g) granulated white sugar

½ cup (110 g) packed dark brown sugar

1 large egg, at room temperature

1 tsp pure vanilla extract

2 tbsp (30 ml) heavy cream

7 tbsp (105 g) Dark Chocolate Ganache (page 178), or store-bought

¼ cup (48 g) chocolate sprinkles

½ cup (85 g) milk chocolate chips

½ cup (85 g) dark chocolate chips

For the chocolate cookie, sift the flour, cocoa powder, baking powder and salt together. Whisk together to ensure they are well combined. Set aside.

Use the paddle attachment on a stand mixer to cream together the butter, shortening and white and brown sugar on medium speed for about 2 to 3 minutes, until fluffy and pale. Reduce the mixer speed to low and add in the egg. Once the egg is incorporated into the mixture, add the vanilla and the cream.

With the mixer speed on low, add in the flour mixture and continue to mix until the cookie dough just comes together.

To assemble the cookies, line a jelly roll pan with parchment paper and use this as your work area.

Divide the cookie dough in half, about 1¼ cups (300 ml) each. Divide each piece in half again, and roll each piece into a ball. Use the palms of your hands to flatten the dough balls into a circle 4 inches (10 cm) in diameter.

Use your fingers or a spoon to gently press into the center of 2 of the flattened cookie circles to create a concave area to hold the chocolate ganache. Divide the ganache between the 2 circles. Top with the other flattened cookie circles and use your fingers to pinch together the top and bottom edges of the cookie and smooth out the sides to create a seamless colossal cookie.

Top each cookie with chocolate sprinkles and milk chocolate and dark chocolate chips. Gently press the chocolate chips onto the dough to set in place. Place the tray with the cookies in the freezer for at least 20 minutes for the dough to rest. Preheat the oven to 350°F (177°C).

Bake one cookie at a time for 22 to 26 minutes. Once the cookie is removed from the oven, allow it to cool down on the baking tray for about 20 minutes before moving it to the cooling rack. If the cookie is moved too soon, it could break apart easily.

Hot Chocolate + Marshmallow

Do you ever crave a giant mug of hot chocolate with an overflowing, never-ending amount of marshmallows? This cookie will be your dream come true.

Yield: 2 colossal cookies

⅓ cup (80 ml) Dark Chocolate Ganache (page 178), or store-bought

⅓ cup (80 ml) marshmallow fluff

1 cup (125 g) all-purpose flour

¼ cup plus 2 tbsp (32 g) unsweetened cocoa powder

½ tsp baking powder

½ tsp baking soda

½ tsp espresso powder

¼ tsp salt

½ cup plus 2 tbsp (142 g) unsalted butter, at room temperature

¾ cup plus 2 tbsp (176 g) granulated white sugar

1 large egg, at room temperature

1 tsp pure vanilla extract

½ cup (85 g) chocolate chips

½ cup (23 g) mini marshmallows

For the chocolate marshmallow filling, whisk the chocolate ganache and marshmallow fluff together and set aside.

For the chocolate cookie, sift together the flour, cocoa, baking powder, baking soda, espresso powder and salt. Whisk the ingredients together to ensure they are well combined.

Using the paddle attachment on a stand mixer, cream together the butter and sugar on medium speed for about 2 to 3 minutes until the mixture is pale and fluffy. Reduce the mixer speed to low, and then add in the egg. Once the egg is incorporated into the mixture, add the vanilla.

With the mixer speed on low, add in the flour mixture and continue to mix until the cookie dough just comes together.

To assemble the cookies, line a jelly roll pan with parchment paper and use this as your work area.

Roll ⅔ cup (160 g) of cookie dough into a ball, and then use the palms of your hands to flatten it into a circle 5 inches (13 cm) in diameter. Repeat 3 times.

Divide the ganache mixture between 2 flattened cookie circles. Gently top with the other flattened cookie circles. Be careful not to press onto the center of the cookie or some of the filling may ooze out from the sides. Use your fingers to pinch together the top and bottom edges of the cookies, and then smooth out the sides for a seamless cookie.

Decorate the cookies by gently pressing the chocolate chips and marshmallows onto the cookies. Place the tray of cookies in the freezer for at least 20 minutes for the cookie dough to rest. Preheat the oven to 350°F (177°C).

Bake one cookie at a time for 22 to 26 minutes, or until a slight crack forms on the edges, which is an indicator that the cookie is ready. Once the cookie is removed from the oven, allow the cookie to cool down on the baking tray for about 15 minutes prior to moving it to the cooling rack. If the cookie is moved too soon, it could easily break apart.

Dulce de Leche Cookie

When I have a box of assorted chocolates, I'm always looking for the chocolate-covered caramels. That chocolate and caramel combination is so incredible. So why not have a fun cookie version? A chocolate cookie with dulce de leche AND sprinkles?! It seems too good to be true, but once you make it you'll believe it.

Yield: 2 colossal cookies

1¼ cups (156 g) all-purpose flour

⅔ cup (33 g) chocolate fudge instant pudding mix

¼ cup (22 g) unsweetened cocoa powder

1 tsp baking soda

¼ tsp salt

½ cup (114 g) unsalted butter, at room temperature

½ cup (110 g) packed dark brown sugar

½ cup (100 g) granulated white sugar

1 large egg, at room temperature

1 tsp pure vanilla extract

2 tbsp (30 ml) heavy cream

¾ cup (128 g) chocolate chips

6 tbsp (90 ml) dulce de leche

⅔ cup (128 g) rainbow sprinkles

Sift together the flour, pudding mix, cocoa, baking soda and salt. Whisk together to ensure they are well combined and set aside.

Use the paddle attachment on a stand mixer to cream together the butter and brown and white sugar on medium speed. After 2 to 3 minutes, the mixture will become fluffy and pale. Reduce the mixer speed to low and add in the egg. Once the egg is incorporated into the mixture, add the vanilla and the cream, allowing each ingredient to be fully incorporated before adding in the next.

With the mixer speed on low, add in the flour mixture. Scrape down the sides of the bowl as needed. Once the cookie dough just comes together, add in the chocolate chips. Continue to mix for a few more seconds until the chips are evenly distributed.

To assemble the cookies, line a jelly roll pan with parchment paper and use this as your work area.

Divide the dough into 4 pieces. Roll each piece into a round ball, and then use the palms of your hands to flatten each ball into a circle 5 inches (13 cm) in diameter.

Use your fingers to gently press into the center area of 2 of the flattened cookie circles to create a small concave area. Divide the dulce de leche between the 2 circles. Place the other flattened cookie circles over the top, but be careful not to press down onto the center. Use your fingers to pinch together the top and bottom edges of the cookie, and then smooth out the sides for a seamless finish.

Top each cookie with rainbow sprinkles. The best method I've come up with is to use a spoon to gently sprinkle the rainbow sprinkles over the cookie dough from the top. Then, I use my hands to cup along the sides of the cookie, and while sprinkling the rainbow sprinkles over the cookie, press them onto the sides of the cookie. Once completed, the entire surface area should be covered with sprinkles. The cookie dough is a little sticky, so the sprinkles will stick to it. Place the tray with the cookies in the freezer for the dough to rest for at least 20 minutes. Preheat the oven to 350°F (177°C).

Bake one cookie at a time for 22 to 26 minutes. You'll know the cookie is ready if the edges have a slight crack. Once the cookie is removed from the oven, allow it to cool down on the baking tray for about 20 minutes prior to moving it to the cooling rack. The warm cookie could break apart easily, especially with the melted dulce de leche in the center.

Chocolate Stuffed with Red Velvet Cookie

Nothing seems to be more romantic than having a combination of chocolate and red velvet, especially when the red velvet is stuffed inside for a fun a surprise! I really love chocolate, and this chocolate cookie is perfect with a light crisp on the outside and the soft red velvet on the inside. The subtle contrast in textures of the chocolatey layers will make anyone's heart skip a beat.

Yield: 4 colossal cookies

CHOCOLATE COOKIE

2 cups (250 g) all-purpose flour

1⅓ cups (115 g) unsweetened cocoa powder

2 tsp (10 g) baking powder

½ tsp salt

1 cup (227 g) unsalted butter, at room temperature

½ cup (103 g) shortening, at room temperature

1 cup (220 g) packed dark brown sugar

1 cup (200 g) granulated white sugar

2 large eggs, at room temperature

2 tsp (10 ml) pure vanilla extract

¼ cup (60 ml) heavy cream

RED VELVET COOKIE

1½ cups (188 g) all-purpose flour

¼ cup (22 g) unsweetened cocoa powder

½ tsp baking powder

½ tsp baking soda

¼ tsp salt

½ cup plus 2 tbsp (142 g) unsalted butter, at room temperature

½ cup (110 g) packed light brown sugar

½ cup (100 g) granulated white sugar

1 large egg, at room temperature

1 tsp pure vanilla extract

2 tbsp (30 ml) heavy cream

2 tbsp (30 ml) red food coloring or gel coloring

For the chocolate cookie, sift together the flour, cocoa powder, baking powder and salt. Whisk the ingredients together to ensure they are well combined and set aside.

Use the paddle attachment on a stand mixer to cream together the butter, shortening and brown and white sugar on medium speed. Mix for 2 to 3 minutes until the mixture becomes pale and fluffy. Reduce the mixer speed to low and add in the eggs, one at a time, followed by the vanilla and the cream.

With the mixer speed on low, add in the flour mixture. Scrape down the sides as needed to ensure the flour at the bottom of bowl is incorporated. Stop once the cookie dough just comes together. Wrap the cookie dough in plastic wrap to prevent it from drying out.

For the red velvet cookie, sift together the flour, cocoa, baking powder, baking soda and salt. Whisk together the ingredients to ensure they are well-combined, and then set aside.

Use the paddle attachment on a stand mixer to cream together the butter and brown and white sugar on medium speed for about 2 to 3 minutes, until the mixture is fluffy and light. Reduce the mixer speed to low and add in the egg, vanilla, cream and red food coloring. Note that you can use half the amount of food coloring recommended to achieve a red color, but I prefer a vibrant red. You can most definitely add in more coloring at the end if you feel the color is too light.

Continuing with the mixer on low, add the flour mixture and mix until the cookie dough just comes together. If you would like a stronger red color, keep the mixer on the lowest speed and add in red coloring a little bit at a time until the color you love is achieved. Be careful not to overmix the dough. If the dough feels too sticky, place it in the refrigerator for 10 to 15 minutes prior to working with it.

To assemble the cookies, line a jelly roll pan with parchment paper and use them as your work area.

In a small bowl mix together the dark, milk and white chocolate chips and set aside.

Divide the chocolate cookie dough into 4 equal parts, about 1¼ cups (300 ml) each. Divide each part in half again, and roll each piece into a ball. Use the palms of your hands to flatten the balls into circles 4½ inches (11 cm) in diameter.

(continued)

Chocolate Stuffed with Red Velvet Cookie (Continued)

ADDITIONAL INGREDIENTS
½ cup (85 g) dark chocolate chips

½ cup (85 g) milk chocolate chips

½ cup (85 g) white chocolate chips

Roll ⅓ cup (80 g) of red velvet cookie dough into a ball, and then use the palms of your hands to flatten it into a circle 3 inches (8 cm) in diameter. Repeat this 3 more times. Place the flattened red velvet cookies in the centers of the chocolate cookie circles. Take the other flattened chocolate cookie circles and place on top of the red velvet. Use your fingers to pinch together the top and bottom edges of the chocolate cookie, and then smooth out the sides for a seamless finish.

Top the cookies with the triple chocolate chip mixture, gently pressing the chips into the cookie to set them in place. Place the tray with the cookies in the freezer for the dough to rest for about 20 minutes. Preheat the oven for 350°F (177°C).

Bake one cookie at a time for 24 to 28 minutes. Once the cookie is removed from the oven, allow it to cool on the baking tray for about 15 minutes prior to moving it to the cooling rack. If moved too soon, the cookie could break easily.

Chocolate Espresso + Red Velvet Cookie

The beauty of this chocolate and red velvet cookie is the mouth-watering sight of all those layers! The hint of espresso makes for an excellent pick-me-up. What makes this cookie even better than the chocolate espresso red velvet combo is . . . it's stuffed with Nutella! Let's just admit it; it's a sexy cookie.

Yield: 3 colossal cookies

CHOCOLATE ESPRESSO COOKIE

1 cup (125 g) all-purpose flour

¼ cup (22 g) unsweetened cocoa powder

1 tsp espresso powder

½ tsp baking soda

¼ tsp salt

½ cup plus 2 tbsp (142 g) unsalted butter, at room temperature

¾ cup (150 g) granulated white sugar

1 large egg, at room temperature

1 tsp pure vanilla extract

2 tbsp (30 ml) heavy cream

½ cup (85 g) chocolate chips

RED VELVET COOKIE

1½ cups (188 g) all-purpose flour

¼ cup (22 g) unsweetened cocoa powder

½ tsp baking powder

½ tsp baking soda

¼ tsp salt

½ cup plus 2 tbsp (142 g) unsalted butter, at room temperature

½ cup (110 g) packed light brown sugar

½ cup (100 g) granulated white sugar

1 large egg, at room temperature

1 tsp pure vanilla extract

2 tbsp (30 ml) heavy cream

2 tbsp (30 ml) red food coloring or gel coloring

For the chocolate espresso cookie, sift together the flour, cocoa, espresso, baking soda and salt. Whisk the ingredients to ensure they are well combined and set aside.

Using the paddle attachment on a stand mixer, cream together the butter and sugar on medium speed for 2 to 3 minutes until it is pale and fluffy. Reduce the mixer speed to low and add in the egg, followed by the vanilla and cream, adding each ingredient after the previous is fully combined into the mixture.

With the mixer speed on low, add in the flour mixture. When the dough just comes together, add in the chocolate chips. Wrap the cookie dough in plastic wrap to prevent it from drying out.

For the red velvet cookie, sift together the flour, cocoa, baking powder, baking soda and salt. Whisk to ensure that they are well combined and set aside.

Using the paddle attachment on a stand mixer, cream together the butter and brown and white sugar on medium speed for 2 to 3 minutes until the mixture becomes fluffy and pale. Reduce the mixer speed to low and add in the egg. Once the egg is incorporated into the mixture, add the vanilla and the cream. Add in the food coloring. I prefer gel food coloring because there is less liquid, and it does not affect the batter as much. Either way the cookies will be absolutely delicious.

With the mixer speed on low, add in the flour mixture until the dough just comes together. If the dough feels too sticky, place it in the refrigerator for 10 to 15 minutes prior to working with it.

To assemble the cookies, line a jelly roll pan with parchment paper and use this as your work area.

Divide the chocolate espresso cookie dough into 6 equal parts. Divide the red velvet cookie dough into 6 equal parts.

Roll each piece of dough into a ball. Take one chocolate espresso and one red velvet dough ball, and press them together to create one cookie dough ball. Roll it together into a larger cookie dough ball, but keep the chocolate cookie dough on one side and the red velvet cookie dough on the other. Using the palms of your hands, flatten the cookie dough into a circle 5 inches (13 cm) in diameter. Make sure the seam between the 2 cookies is in the middle so the cookie is one-half chocolate espresso and one-half red velvet.

(continued)

Chocolate Espresso + Red Velvet Cookie (Continued)

ADDITIONAL INGREDIENTS

¾ cup (180 g) chocolate-hazelnut spread (I prefer Nutella)

¾ cup (128 g) dark chocolate chips

¾ cup (128 g) white chocolate chips

Divide the chocolate-hazelnut spread among 3 cookie circles, and then place the other flattened cookie circle on top. Use your fingers to pinch together the top and bottom edges of the cookie, and then smooth out the sides for a seamless finish.

Place the dark chocolate chips on the chocolate-espresso sides of the cookies and white chocolate chips on the red velvet sides. Feel free to take on some creative freedom and mix it up or randomly place the chocolate chips.

Place the tray of cookies in the freezer for at least 20 minutes for the cookie dough to rest. Preheat the oven for 350°F (177°C).

Bake one cookie at a time for 24 to 28 minutes. Once the cookie is removed from the oven, allow it to cool on the baking sheet for about 20 minutes. If the cookie is moved too soon to the cooling rack, it could break apart easily.

Mexican Hot Chocolate

The combination of chocolate, cinnamon and spicy cayenne gives this cookie a warmth similar to what you get from drinking hot chocolate. The crispy edges of the cookie make for the perfect contrast with the gooey marshmallow inside. One of the best parts is breaking off pieces from the cookie and seeing the stretchy marshmallow pull!

If you like a little spicier kick in these cookies, use 3 or even 4 dashes of cayenne pepper!

Yield: 2 colossal cookies

1 cup (125 g) all-purpose flour

½ cup (43 g) unsweetened cocoa powder

½ tsp baking powder

¼ tsp salt

1 tsp ground cinnamon

1 dash ground nutmeg

2 to 3 dashes ground cayenne pepper

½ cup plus 2 tbsp (142 g) unsalted butter

1 cup (100 g) granulated white sugar

1 large egg, at room temperature

1 tsp pure vanilla extract

⅔ cup plus ½ cup (53 g) mini marshmallows, divided

½ cup (85 g) chocolate chips

Sift together the flour, cocoa, baking powder, salt, cinnamon, nutmeg and cayenne pepper. Whisk together to ensure they are well combined and set aside.

Use the paddle attachment on a stand mixer to cream together the butter and sugar on medium speed for about 3 to 4 minutes until the mixture is light and fluffy. Reduce the mixer speed to low and then add in the egg. Once the egg is incorporated into the mixture, add the vanilla.

Continue with the mixer speed on low and add in the flour mixture. Stop the mixer once the cookie dough just comes together.

To assemble the cookies, line a jelly roll pan with parchment paper and use this as your work area.

Divide the cookie dough into 4 equal pieces. Roll each piece into a ball, and then use the palms of your hands to flatten each ball into a circle 5 inches (13 cm) in diameter.

Place ⅓ cup (15 g) of mini marshmallows in the centers of 2 of the flattened cookie circles and top with the remaining 2 cookie circles. Use your fingers to pinch together the top and bottom edges of the cookie, and then smooth out the sides for a seamless finish.

Cover the cookies with chocolate chips and mini marshmallows, and gently press them onto the cookie to set it in place. Put the tray with the cookies in the freezer for the dough to rest for at least 20 minutes. Preheat the oven to 350°F (177°C).

Bake one cookie at a time for 22 to 26 minutes. Once the cookie is out from the oven, allow it to cool down on the baking tray for about 15 minutes prior to moving it to the cooling rack, otherwise it could easily break apart—especially with the soft marshmallow center.

If you have a kitchen torch, add a little smoky campfire touch to the marshmallows on top by torching them a little bit.

Rocky Road Cookie

Rocky road brings back memories of my childhood when my friends and I would have ice cream parties and scream at the top of our lungs, "I scream, you scream, we ALL scream for ICE CREAM!!" I love rocky road ice cream for its perfect combination of chocolate, nuts and marshmallows. With that, and my evolving love of cookies, I had to create a cookie that would instantly bring me back to my childhood. The marshmallow stuffing in the cookie will really rock your world!

Yield: 2 colossal cookies

1¼ cups (156 g) all-purpose flour

⅔ cup (33 g) chocolate fudge instant pudding mix

¼ cup (22 g) unsweetened cocoa powder

1 tsp baking soda

¼ tsp salt

½ cup (114 g) unsalted butter, at room temperature

½ cup (110 g) packed dark brown sugar

½ cup (100 g) granulated white sugar

1 large egg, at room temperature

1 tsp pure vanilla extract

2 tbsp (30 ml) heavy cream

⅔ cup plus ½ cup (53 g) mini marshmallows, divided

⅔ cup (87 g) coarsely chopped mixed nuts

½ cup (85 g) chocolate chips

Sift together the flour, pudding mix, cocoa, baking soda and salt. Whisk the ingredients together to ensure that all the components are well combined and set aside.

Use the paddle attachment on a stand mixer to cream together the butter and brown and white sugar on medium speed for about 2 to 3 minutes until the mixture is fluffy and pale. Reduce the mixer speed to low and add in the egg. Once the egg is incorporated into the mixture, add the vanilla and the cream.

With the mixer speed on low, add in the flour mixture. Mix until the cookie dough just comes together.

To assemble the cookies, line a jelly roll pan with parchment paper and use this as your work area.

Roll ⅔ cup (160 g) of cookie dough into a ball, and then use the palms of your hands to flatten it into a circle 4½ inches (11 cm) in diameter. Repeat 3 more times.

Use your fingers to gently press into the center of 2 of the flattened cookie circles to create a small concave area to hold the marshmallows. Place ⅓ cup (15 g) of marshmallows on these circles. Place the other flattened cookie dough over the marshmallows. Use your fingers to pinch together the top and bottom edges of the cookie, and then smooth out the sides for a seamless finish.

In a small bowl mix together the remaining marshmallows, the nuts and the chocolate chips. Use the mixed toppings to cover the entire top surface of the cookies. Gently press them onto the dough to set it in place.

Place the tray with the cookies in the freezer for at least 20 minutes for the cookie dough to rest. Preheat the oven to 350°F (177°C).

Bake one cookie at a time for 22 to 26 minutes. There are two ways to check for whether the cookie is done baking: first, the edges should have slight cracks, and second, the dome-shaped part of the cookie should be flattened on top and the center of the dough should have a light crisp to it. Once the cookie is removed from the oven, allow it to cool down for about 15 minutes prior to moving it to the cooling rack. If moved too soon, the cookie could easily break apart.

Sugar Rush!

There is nothing more painful than that afternoon slump when you just need a pick-me-up to get yourself through the rest of the day. Or those moments when the morning tea or coffee is just not doing it for you. My solution has always been to have one of these cookies for a sugar rush. Sometimes you really just need some extra sugar to get yourself going, which is why I love the cookies in this chapter.

Rainbow Fruity Cereal + Marshmallow Cookies

This cookie always puts a wide-eyed, giant ear-to-ear smile on my face and makes me feel like I just won the lottery. It reminds of me of when I was a kid, and the Fruity Pebbles cereal was always considered to be a treat. Now, as an adult, I get to have it whenever I want, AND I get to add marshmallows to it! The texture of the cookie is soft, and the marshmallow gooey, and the sweet Fruity Pebbles cereal crispy. It just makes my inner-kid dreams come true!

Yield: 2 colossal cookies

1¼ cups (156 g) all-purpose flour

¼ cup (13 g) vanilla instant pudding mix

½ tsp baking soda

¼ tsp salt

7 tbsp (98 g) unsalted butter, at room temperature

2 tbsp (26 g) shortening, at room temperature

½ cup (100 g) granulated white sugar

½ cup (110 g) packed light brown sugar

1 large egg, at room temperature

½ tsp pure vanilla extract

1¾ cups (70 g) Fruity Pebbles cereal, divided

⅔ cup (30 g) mini marshmallows

Whisk together the flour, pudding mix, baking soda and salt and set aside.

Using the paddle attachment on a stand mixer, cream together the butter and shortening with the white and brown sugar on medium speed. After 2 to 3 minutes, the mixture will become light and fluffy. Reduce the mixer speed to low and add in the egg. Once the egg is incorporated into the mixture, add the vanilla.

With the mixer speed on low, add in the flour mixture. Once the cookie dough just comes together, add in the cereal and continue to mix for only a few more seconds. Don't mix for too long or the cereal will be crushed to bits!

To assemble the cookies, line a jelly roll pan with parchment paper and use this as your work area.

Divide the cookie dough into 4 equal pieces. Roll each piece into a ball, and then use the palms of your hands to flatten it into a circle 5 inches (13 cm) in diameter.

Use your fingers to gently press into the center of 2 of the flattened cookie circles to create a small concave area, and place ⅓ cup (15 g) of marshmallows in the center of each. The concave area will help hold the mini marshmallows. Place the other flattened cookie circles on top of the marshmallows. Use your fingers to pinch together the top and bottom edges of the cookie to create a seal, and then smooth out the sides for a seamless finish. It is important to create a seal without visible seams, because the marshmallows will expand while baking and could break the seams and ooze out.

Place the remaining cereal in a bowl and roll the cookies around in the cereal to create a colorful shell.

Place the tray with the cookies in the freezer for at least 20 minutes for the dough to rest before baking. Preheat the oven to 350°F (177°C).

Bake one cookie at a time for 22 to 26 minutes, or until edges are a light golden-brown. Once the cookie is removed from the oven, allow it to cool down on the baking tray for about 15 minutes to avoid breaking it when moving to the cooling rack.

Strawberry Sugar Cookie

With freeze-dried berries and fruits becoming even more popular, I decided to turn freeze-dried strawberries into a powder and mix it with sugar to make strawberry sugar. Then I took the strawberry sugar and made it into a sugar cookie. TA-DA, I present to you the strawberry sugar cookie! But of course, you need it stuffed with strawberry jam to make it that much better.

Yield: 2 colossal cookies

1 cup (20 g) freeze-dried strawberries

¾ cup (150 g) granulated white sugar

1 cup plus 2 tbsp (143 g) all-purpose flour

½ tsp baking soda

¼ tsp salt

½ cup plus 2 tbsp (142 g) unsalted butter, at room temperature

1 large egg, at room temperature

1 tsp pure vanilla extract

1 tsp red gel food coloring (optional)

6 tbsp (90 ml) strawberry preserve

¼ cup (48 g) sand sugar (optional)

Make the strawberry sugar by pulsing the freeze-dried strawberries and sugar in a food processor until the freeze-dried strawberries are a fine powder. Be careful when you open the lid to the food processor because a strawberry sugar cloud will float out.

For the sugar cookie, whisk together the flour, baking soda and salt and set aside.

Use the paddle attachment on a stand mixer to cream together the strawberry sugar and butter on medium speed. After 3 to 4 minutes, the mixture will become a light pink color and fluffy.

Reduce the mixer speed to low and add in the egg. Once the egg is incorporated into the mixture, add the vanilla. If you would like to use food coloring for a more vibrant and distinct red color, add it now. Without food coloring the color of the baked cookie will be a light pink with a hint of brown.

With the mixer speed on low, add in the flour mixture and stop the mixer when the cookie dough just comes together.

To assemble the cookies, line a jelly roll pan with parchment paper and use this as your work area.

Divide the cookie dough into 4 equal pieces. Roll each piece into a ball, and then use the palms of your hands to flatten them into circles 4 inches (10 cm) in diameter.

Next, use your fingers to gently press into the center of 2 of the flattened cookies to create a concave area to hold the strawberry preserve. Divide the preserves between the 2 cookie circles. Gently place the other flattened cookie dough on top of the preserves. Do not press down on the center or the preserves could leak out. Use your fingers to pinch together the top and bottom edges of the cookie, and then smooth out the sides to create a seamless finish.

An optional finishing touch is to sprinkle 2 tablespoons (6 g) of sand sugar on top of each cookie to create a nice texture. Place the tray with the cookies in the freezer and allow the dough to rest for at least 20 minutes. Preheat the oven to 350°F (177°C).

Bake one cookie at a time for 20 to 24 minutes, or until the edges are light golden brown–pink color. Allow the cookie to cool down on the baking tray for about 20 to 25 minutes before moving it to the cooling rack as the cookie can break apart easily if moved too soon. The melted strawberry preserve makes this cookie extra delicate, so handle with care.

Tie-Dye Sugar Cookie

If you need a cookie for a kid's birthday party, this cookie is kid approved! With a sugar cookie base, you can let your imagination run wild with your favorite color combinations to swirl together. The swirl of tie-dye colors is always exciting and to make it even more extraordinary, the center is filled with a sprinkle surprise! When the kids break this cookie open, they'll love that they're being showered with sprinkles. Get ready for endless laughter and fun going through the roof!

For the coloring, have some fun and change the colors to your own favorite combinations. I used the least amount of coloring for green to have a lighter green color, because green is so similar to blue. The pink is a bright pop of color and the purple contrasts nicely with the pink and complements the blue. I hope you have fun playing with the color combinations!

Yield: 3 colossal cookies

2¼ cups (281 g) all-purpose flour

½ tsp baking powder

¼ tsp salt

1 cup (227 g) unsalted butter, at room temperature

1½ cup (300 g) granulated white sugar

1 large egg, at room temperature

½ tbsp (8 ml) pure vanilla extract

¼ tsp blue food coloring

½ tsp hot pink food coloring

½ tsp purple food coloring

1 drop green and 1 drop yellow food coloring

½ cup plus 1 tbsp (108 g) favorite sprinkles

Whisk together the flour, baking powder and salt and set aside.

Use the paddle attachment on a stand mixer to cream together the butter and sugar on medium speed. After 3 to 4 minutes, the mixture will become fluffy and light. Reduce the mixer speed to low, and add in the egg. Once the egg is incorporated into the mixture, add the vanilla.

With the mixer speed on low, add in the flour mixture and continue to mix until the cookie dough just comes together. Separate the cookie dough into 4 equal parts.

To color the dough, place one piece back into the mixer and add the blue food coloring. You can slowly add in drops of food coloring until the desired color is reached, or add all the recommended amount. Once the color is evenly distributed into the cookie, stop the mixer to avoid overmixing. Wash the bowl and paddle attachment before moving on to the next color.

Repeat the above steps for the pink, purple and green colored dough. If you do not have hot pink food coloring, red food coloring will work. If you do not have purple food coloring, use twice the number of red drops as blue; for example, if you add 10 drops of red food coloring, then add 5 drops of blue food coloring. For the green colored dough, I used one drop of green and one drop of yellow for a brighter green color, but feel free to play with different combinations.

To assemble the cookies, line a jelly roll pan with parchment paper and use this as your work area.

Divide each colored dough in half. Roll each piece into a stick about 12 inches (30 cm) long. Line 4 different colored sticks together in a row, and then roll them together to become one larger log. Repeat to form 2 logs. Starting from one end of a log, twist the dough. Continue to work your way across the entire log, and in the end you'll have a log of colors swirled together. Note that the tighter the twist, the finer the tie-dye swirls will be in the cookie.

Once you have 2 logs of swirled dough, divide each one into 3 equal pieces (about ¼ cup [60 g] for each piece).

(continued)

Roll each colored piece of dough into a stick that is 12 inches (30 cm) long.

Make one large log by twisting the 4 colors together. Repeat to make 2 logs.

Divide each log into 3 parts and flatten in 3 circles. Create a concave area and load in the sprinkles.

Place the other flattened dough on top and pinch the sides to seal.

Tie-Dye Sugar Cookie (Continued)

Roll each piece into a ball, and then flatten each ball into a circle 4 inches (10 cm) in diameter. When the dough is flattened, the tie-dye of swirls becomes more pronounced.

Look at the flattened cookie circles and pick the 3 tie-dyed sides that you like the most for the top of the cookie. For the bottom circles, use your fingers to gently press down onto the center to create a concave area to hold the sprinkles. Divide the sprinkles among the 3 bottom circles. Place the other flattened cookie dough on top and use your fingers to pinch together the top and bottom edges of the cookie, and then smooth out the sides for a seamless finish.

Place the tray with the cookies in the freezer and allow the dough to rest for at least 20 minutes. Preheat the oven to 350°F (177°C).

Bake one cookie at a time for 20 to 24 minutes, or until the edges are light golden-brown. Once the cookie is out of the oven, allow it to cool down on the baking tray for about 10 minutes before moving it to the cooling rack. If moved too soon, it could cause the cookie to break apart.

TIE-DYE SUGAR COOKIES STUFFED WITH MARSHMALLOW VARIATION: Play with different tie-dye color combinations and stuff it with marshmallow! All you need is 3 tablespoons (45 ml) of marshmallow fluff. Or, to keep the cookie stuffed with sprinkles and marshmallow, use 2 tablespoons (30 ml) of marshmallow fluff on the bottom layer, and then top with 1 tablespoon (12 g) of your favorite sprinkles. Let's take this to the next level of fun!

Red Velvet Stuffed with Chocolate Chip Cookie

My love for red velvet started from the very first time I ever had a piece of red velvet cake. So of course, we need to have a red velvet cookie—but not just any red velvet cookie! This one is stuffed with a chocolate chip cookie. As with all stuffed cookies, one may call the chocolate chip a fun surprise, but in this case, for me, this is definitely a necessary combination.

Yield: 2 colossal cookies

RED VELVET COOKIE

1½ cups (188 g) all-purpose flour

¼ cup (22 g) unsweetened cocoa powder

½ tsp baking powder

½ tsp baking soda

¼ tsp salt

½ cup plus 2 tbsp (142 g) unsalted butter, at room temperature

½ cup (110 g) packed light brown sugar

½ cup (100 g) granulated white sugar

1 large egg, at room temperature

1 tsp pure vanilla extract

2 tbsp (30 ml) buttermilk

2 tbsp (30 ml) red food coloring or gel coloring

CHOCOLATE CHIP COOKIE

1¼ cups (156 g) all-purpose flour

1 tsp baking powder

¼ tsp salt

½ cup (114 g) unsalted butter, at room temperature

¾ cup (165 g) packed light brown sugar

¼ cup (50 g) granulated white sugar

1 large egg, at room temperature

1 tsp pure vanilla extract

½ cup (85 g) chocolate chips

ADDITIONAL INGREDIENTS

⅔ cup (113 g) white chocolate chips

For the red velvet cookie, sift together the flour, cocoa, baking powder, baking soda and salt. Whisk together to ensure the ingredients are well combined and set aside.

Use the paddle attachment on a stand mixer to cream together the butter and brown and white sugar for 2 to 3 minutes on medium speed until the mixture becomes fluffy and pale. Reduce the mixer speed to low and add in the egg. Once the egg is incorporated into the mixture, add the vanilla and the buttermilk, allowing each ingredient to be fully incorporated before adding the next.

Add in the red food coloring. You can start by adding a little bit at a time until you reach the desired color. The color will be lighter after adding in the flour mixture, but more red food coloring can be added at the end after the cookie dough comes together.

With the mixer speed on low, add in the flour mixture and continue to mix until the cookie dough just comes together. Add in more food coloring now if desired. Wrap the dough in plastic wrap to prevent drying. If the dough feels too sticky, place it in the refrigerator for 10 to 15 minutes prior to working with it.

For the chocolate chip cookie, whisk together the flour, baking powder and salt and set aside.

Use the paddle attachment on a stand mixer to cream together the butter and brown and white sugar on medium speed for about 2 to 3 minutes until the mixture is fluffy and light. Reduce the mixer speed to low and add in the egg, followed by the vanilla.

With the mixer speed on low, add in the flour mixture and continue to mix until the cookie dough just comes together. Add in the chocolate chips.

To assemble the cookies, line a jelly roll pan with parchment paper and use this as your work area.

Roll ⅔ cup (160 g) of red velvet cookie dough into a ball. Use the palms of your hands to flatten it into a circle 5 inches (13 cm) in diameter. Repeat to have 4 flattened round red velvet cookie circles.

Roll ⅓ cup (80 g) of chocolate chip cookie dough into a ball. Use the palms of your hands to flatten it into a circle 3 inches (8 cm) in diameter. Repeat to form another chocolate chip cookie dough circle. Place the chocolate chip cookie dough in the center of one of the flattened red velvet cookie circles and place the other red velvet cookie dough on top. Use your fingers to pinch together the top and bottom edges of the red velvet cookie, and then smooth out the sides for a seamless stuffed red velvet cookie! Repeat for the second cookie.

Cover each cookie with half of the white chocolate chips. Gently press the chocolate chips onto the cookie to set in place. Place the tray with the cookies in the freezer for the cookie dough to rest for at least 20 minutes. Preheat the oven to 350°F (177°C).

Bake one cookie at a time for 24 to 28 minutes, or until the edges are golden-brown. Once the cookie is out of the oven, be sure to allow it to cool down on the baking tray for about 15 minutes prior to moving it to the cooling rack.

Espresso Shortbread

If you need a mid-day pick-me-up, this cookie will be your new best friend. When an afternoon coffee might be a little too much, this could be just what you need. The contrast of the crumbly espresso shortbread and soft chocolate ganache balances nicely together. But, that's not all; the mocha glaze on top just makes this a quintessential treat.

Yield: 2 colossal cookies

2 cups (250 g) all-purpose flour

2 tsp (4 g) espresso powder

Pinch of salt

1 cup (227 g) unsalted butter, at room temperature

1 cup (120 g) sifted powdered sugar, divided

1 tsp pure vanilla extract

6 tbsp (90 ml) Dark Chocolate Ganache (page 178) or store-bought

2 tbsp (11 g) unsweetened cocoa powder

2 tbsp (30 ml) brewed espresso (you can use reconstituted espresso powder)

For the shortbread, whisk together the flour, espresso powder and pinch of salt and set aside.

Use the paddle attachment on a stand mixer to cream together the butter and ½ cup (60 g) of powdered sugar on low speed. When the sugar and butter are mixed together, increase the mixer speed to medium and mix for about 2 to 3 minutes, until the mixture is fluffy and light. Reduce the mixer speed to low and add in the vanilla.

With the mixer speed on low, add in the flour mixture and stop the mixer once the cookie dough just comes together. I love seeing the little specks of espresso in the cookie dough, which makes it so pretty!

To assemble the cookies, line a jelly roll pan with parchment paper and use this as your work area.

Divide the cookie dough 4 equal pieces. Roll each piece into a ball, and then use the palms of your hands to flatten each ball into a circle 4½ inches (11 cm) in diameter. Use your fingers to gently press into the centers of 2 circles to create a concave area for the ganache. Divide the ganache between the 2 circles. Place the other flattened cookie circles on top. Use your fingers to pinch together the top and bottom edges of the cookie, and then smooth out the sides for a seamless finish.

Place the tray with the cookies in the freezer for at least 20 minutes for the cookie dough to rest. Preheat the oven to 350°F (177°C).

Bake one cookie at a time for 22 to 26 minutes, or until edges are light golden-brown. Allow the cookie to cool down for about 20 minutes on the baking tray before moving it to the cooling rack, otherwise it could break apart easily.

While the cookies are baking, make the mocha chocolate glaze! You can use the same espresso powder as for the cookie, just brew it according to the instructions. In a medium-size bowl, whisk together ½ cup (60 g) of powdered sugar, cocoa and brewed espresso. Continue to whisk until the mixture comes together and becomes a glaze. Set the glaze to the side. Once the cookies have cooled down, use the whisk to drizzle the glaze over the shortbread!

Lemon Shortbread

If you love lemon desserts such as lemon bars and cakes, you'll love this cookie! The buttery shortbread has a hint of lemon flavor from the lemon zest, but what makes it irresistible is the lemon curd on the inside! The sweet and tart, creamy, flavorful lemon curd with its beautifully vibrant yellow color screams happiness and excitement. I couldn't help but eat an entire one on my own after I made it!

Yield: 2 colossal cookies

1 cup (227 g) unsalted butter, at room temperature

⅔ cup plus 2 tbsp (159 g) granulated white sugar

1 tbsp (15 g) lemon zest (about 2 lemons), divided

2 tbsp (30 ml) fresh lemon juice (about 1 lemon)

2 cups (250 g) all-purpose flour

6 tbsp (90 ml) Lemon Curd (page 182), or store-bought

For the shortbread cookie, using the paddle attachment on a stand mixer, cream together the butter and sugar on medium speed. Continue to mix for 3 to 4 minutes, until the mixture is fluffy and light.

Reduce the mixer speed to low and add in 2 teaspoons (10 g) of lemon zest and the juice. Add in the flour and continue to mix until the cookie dough just comes together.

To assemble the cookies, line a jelly roll pan with parchment paper and use this as your work area.

Divide the cookie dough into 4 equal pieces. Roll each piece into a ball, and then use the palms of your hands to flatten each ball into a circle 4 inches (10 cm) in diameter.

Set 2 of the flattened cookie circles on the parchment paper and use your fingers to gently press into the center of the cookie to create a concave area in the middle that is 2 inches (6 cm) in diameter and slightly deep. These 2 cookies will be used for the bottoms of the cookies, and the concave area is an important element to hold the lemon curd later on. Place the bottoms in the freezer for 10 minutes. Preheat the oven to 350°F (177°C).

Place the 2 cookies on opposite ends of the baking sheet, leaving a few inches from the edge of the baking sheet, and bake for 10 minutes. The cookie will spread out a little bit while baking, but both cookies can be baked together.

Remove the cookie bottoms from the oven and divide the lemon curd between them. Place the unbaked, flattened cookie dough over the top of the partially baked cookies. It's important to be careful, as the bottom halves are hot. Gently smooth out the cookie dough from the top half of the cookies to the bottom half and cover as much of the base of the bottom half of the cookies as possible. Place the cookies back in the oven to bake for 15 to 18 minutes, or until the edges are golden-brown.

The reason for the two-part baking is to partially bake the base of the cookie to hold the lemon curd without it leaking through the bottom of the cookie. Once the cookies are removed from the oven, allow them to cool down on the baking tray for at least 30 minutes before moving it to a cooling rack, as they are quite fragile. Sprinkle the remaining lemon zest over each cookie.

LEMON SHORTBREAD STUFFED WITH BLUEBERRY PRESERVES VARIATION: I love a great blueberry pie and this is a perfect cookie version of it. Instead of using lemon curd, substitute 3 tablespoons (45 ml) of blueberry preserves for each cookie. Follow the same instructions for the cookie dough assembly, baking and cooling.

Blueberry and Cream Cookie

Blueberries and cream reminds me of having vanilla ice cream with fresh blueberries on top, which is exactly what this cookie is. The vanilla pudding mix and sweetened condensed milk adds a creamy sweetness that makes this cookie incredibly delicious. The blueberry preserves packs in the blueberry flavor for this cookie.

Yield: 2 colossal cookies

1½ cups (188 g) all-purpose flour

¼ cup (13 g) vanilla instant pudding mix

½ tsp baking powder

¼ tsp salt

½ cup (114 g) unsalted butter, at room temperature

½ cup (110 g) packed light brown sugar

1 large egg, at room temperature

1 tsp pure vanilla extract

3 tbsp (45 ml) sweetened condensed milk

½ cup (80 g) dried blueberries

⅓ cup (57 g) plus ½ cup (85 g) white chocolate chips, divided

6 tbsp (90 ml) blueberry preserves

Whisk the flour, pudding mix, baking powder and salt together and set aside.

Use the paddle attachment on a stand mixer to cream together the butter and sugar for about 2 to 3 minutes until the mixture becomes fluffy and light. Reduce the mixer speed to low and add in the egg. Once the egg is incorporated into the mixture, add the vanilla and the milk.

With the mixer speed on low, add in the flour mixture and allow the cookie dough to just come together. Add in the dried blueberries and white chocolate chips and continue to mix for a few more seconds.

To assemble the cookies, line a jelly roll pan with parchment paper and use this as your work area.

Divide the cookie dough into 4 equal pieces. Roll each piece into a ball and use the palms of your hands to flatten it into a circle 4½ inches (11 cm) in diameter.

Use your fingers to gently press into the center of 2 of the flattened circles to create a concave area to hold the blueberry preserves. Divide the preserves between the 2 cookies. Place the other circles over the preserves. To prevent oozing, be careful to not press down on the center area where the preserves are. Use your fingers to pinch together the top and bottom edges of the cookies, and then smooth out the sides for a seamless finish.

Cover the tops of the cookies with the remaining white chocolate chips and gently press them in place. Place the cookies in the freezer for at least 20 minutes for the cookie dough to rest. Preheat the oven to 350°F (177°C).

Bake one cookie at a time for 24 to 28 minutes, or until the edges are golden-brown. Once removed from the oven, allow the cookie to cool down on the baking tray for about 30 minutes before moving to the cooling rack to prevent breakage.

BLUEBERRY AND CREAM STUFFED WITH MARSHMALLOW VARIATION:
If you're a marshmallow lover like me, then definitely make this version by adding marshmallow fluff. You'll be on marshmallow cloud nine! Follow the same instructions for the Blueberry and Cream Cookie, but for the stuffing use 2 tablespoons (30 ml) of marshmallow fluff for the bottom topped with 1 tablespoon (15 ml) of blueberry preserves for each cookie. The combination of blueberry and marshmallow is so heavenly.

Oatmeal and Fruit Breakfast Cookies

Breakfast is often cited as the most important meal of the day, but, "What are we supposed to be eating for breakfast?" is open to interpretation. Well, I definitely believe in cookies for breakfast because I have the rest of the day to burn off the calories! And if that's not a good enough excuse, then hopefully knowing that the Oatmeal and Fruit Breakfast Cookies recipes all contain some sort of fiber to jump-start your day helps. Whether the recipe calls for oatmeal, fruit or both, these cookies have you covered for a fantastic start to your morning, but more importantly, give you the energy to take on whatever is coming your way that day!

Apple, Oatmeal + Cinnamon

Oatmeal, a common breakfast item, adds in the fiber and protein needed for the most important meal of the day! For myself, and I think for most of us, oatmeal can be a little bland just on its own, but when mixed with a little bit of this and that, it becomes something that we all love. So with this recipe, the oatmeal, cinnamon and diced apple incorporated into the cookie and the crispy crumble on top will not just be any breakfast cookie, but will definitely remind you of Grandma's famous apple pie. An added bonus—you'll have this amazing cinnamon aroma in your kitchen.

Yield: 2 colossal cookies

APPLE CINNAMON OATMEAL COOKIE

1½ cups (188 g) all-purpose flour

¾ tsp ground cinnamon

½ tsp baking soda

½ tsp salt

½ cup (114 g) unsalted butter, at room temperature

¾ cup (165 g) packed dark brown sugar

¼ cup (50 g) granulated white sugar

1 large egg, at room temperature

1 tbsp (15 ml) maple syrup

1 tsp pure vanilla extract

1⅔ cups (134 g) instant oatmeal

½ cup (55 g) finely diced apple mixed with a dash of cinnamon and a squeeze of fresh lemon juice

CINNAMON CRUMBLE

½ cup (63 g) all-purpose flour

¼ cup (55 g) packed dark brown sugar

½ tsp ground cinnamon

⅛ tsp salt

4 tbsp (57 g) unsalted butter, cold and cut into cubes

Whisk together the flour, cinnamon, baking soda and salt and set aside.

Use the paddle attachment on a stand mixer to cream together the butter and the brown and white sugar on medium speed for about 2 to 3 minutes until light and fluffy. Reduce the mixer speed to low, and add in the egg and mix until fully incorporated. Then add the maple syrup, which gives a subtle caramel aroma to the cookie, followed by the vanilla.

With the mixer speed on low, add in the flour mixture. Once the cookie dough just comes together, add in the oats and mix for a few more seconds.

Use a spatula to fold in the apples. Do not use the mixer for this step because it will crush the crisp texture.

For the crumble, use the paddle attachment on a stand mixer to mix the flour, sugar, cinnamon, salt and butter together on medium-low speed. The key is the cold butter, which will create a nice crumbly texture. Once the mixture comes together, stop the mixer.

To assemble the cookies, line a jelly roll pan with parchment paper and use this as your work area.

Divide the cookie dough in half. Roll each piece into a ball, and then use the palms of your hands to flatten the dough into a circle about 5 inches (13 cm) in diameter and 1 inch (2.5 cm) thick.

Press a generous handful of crumble on top of each cookie. Feel free to pile extra crumble on top, which makes for an extra crispy bonus!

Place the cookies in the freezer to allow the cookie dough to rest for at least 20 minutes. Preheat the oven to 350°F (177°C).

Bake one cookie at a time for 18 to 20 minutes, or until the edges are golden-brown. Allow the cookie to cool down on the baking tray for about 15 minutes prior to moving it to cooling rack. It can break apart easily if moved too soon.

Blueberry Maple Oatmeal

Warm oatmeal with blueberries and almonds makes the perfect combination for a breakfast cookie. The antioxidants and fiber are just an added bonus! I highly recommend warming up this cookie in the oven or microwave to really enjoy the combination of warm oatmeal and the sweet caramel aroma from the maple syrup. This breakfast cookie will remind you of that popular blueberry pie from the little bakery in the next town over, but without the travel time.

Yield: 2 colossal cookies

1 cup (125 g) all-purpose flour

½ tsp baking soda

½ tsp salt

½ cup (114 g) unsalted butter, at room temperature

¾ cup (165 g) packed light brown sugar

¼ cup (50 g) granulated white sugar

1 large egg, at room temperature

1 tbsp (15 ml) maple syrup

1 tsp pure vanilla extract

1⅓ cups (107 g) instant oatmeal

¾ cup (108) sliced almonds, divided

½ cup (80 g) dried blueberries

6 tbsp (90 ml) blueberry preserves

Whisk together the flour, baking soda and salt and set aside.

Use the paddle attachment on a stand mixer to cream together the butter and brown and white sugar on medium speed for 2 to 3 minutes until the mixture is fluffy and light. Reduce the mixer speed to low, and add in the egg. Once the egg is incorporated into the mixture, add the maple syrup and vanilla.

With the mixer speed on low, add in the flour mixture and mix until the cookie dough just comes together. Add in the oatmeal, ½ cup (72 g) of almond slices and the dried blueberries. Allow the mixer to continue for a few more seconds until the ingredients are evenly distributed.

To assemble the cookies, line a jelly roll pan with parchment paper and use this as your work area.

Roll ⅔ cup (160 g) of cookie dough into a ball, and then use the palms of your hands to flatten it into a circle 4½ inches (11 cm) in diameter. Repeat this step so you have 4 flattened cookie circles. Use your fingers to gently press into the center of 2 of the circles to create a concave area to hold the blueberry preserves. Divide the preserves between the 2 cookies. Place the other flattened cookie dough on top. Use your fingers to pinch together the top and bottom edges of the cookie, and then smooth out the sides to create a seamless finish.

Top the cookies with the remaining almond slices. Gently press the slices onto the dough to set in place. Place the tray with the cookies in the freezer for at least 20 minutes to allow the dough to rest. Preheat the oven to 375°F (190°C).

Bake one cookie at a time for 24 to 28 minutes, or until the edges are golden-brown. Once the cookie is removed from the oven, allow it to cool down on the baking tray for at least 15 minutes before moving it to the cooling rack, otherwise it may break apart.

Roasted Banana, Nuts + Oatmeal

If you love roasted banana muffins or a banana and peanut butter combo, this is the breakfast cookie for you! The combination of the caramelized banana, mixed nuts plus peanut butter yields a phenomenal breakfast cookie or a snack from heaven. Needless to say, you're getting some great nutrients along the way.

Yield: 2 colossal cookies

1 cup (125 g) all-purpose flour

½ tsp baking soda

½ tsp ground cinnamon

½ tsp salt

¼ tsp ground nutmeg

½ cup (114 g) unsalted butter, at room temperature

¾ cup (165 g) packed light brown sugar

2 tbsp (26 g) granulated white sugar

1 large egg, at room temperature

1 tsp pure vanilla extract

¾ cup (180 g) mashed Roasted Bananas (page 183)

2 cups (160 g) instant oatmeal

1⅔ cup (218 g) coarsely chopped mixed nuts, divided

⅔ cup (160 g) peanut butter

For the oatmeal cookie, whisk together the flour, baking soda, cinnamon, salt, and nutmeg and set aside.

Use the paddle attachment on a stand mixer to cream together the butter and brown and white sugar on medium speed for 2 to 3 minutes until the mixture is pale and fluffy. Reduce the mixer speed to low, and add in the egg. Once the egg is incorporated into the mixture, add the vanilla and the bananas. With the mixer speed on low, add in the flour mixture and continue to mix until the cookie dough just comes together. Add in the oatmeal and 1 cup (131 g) of nuts, and continue to mix for a few more seconds. If the dough feels too sticky, place it in the refrigerator for 10 to 15 minutes prior to working with it.

To assemble the cookies, line a jelly roll pan with parchment paper and use this as your work area. Roll 1 cup (240 g) of cookie dough into a ball, and then use the palms of your hands to flatten it to a circle 5 inches (13 cm) in diameter. Repeat this step so you have 4 flattened dough circles.

Divide the peanut butter between 2 cookie dough circles and spread it in a 3-inch (8-cm) circle in the center of each. Place the other flattened cookie dough circle on top, covering the peanut butter. Use your fingers to pinch together the top and bottom edges of the cookies, and then smooth out the sides to create a seamless colossal cookie. Cover the cookies with the remaining nuts, and gently press in place. Place the tray with the cookies in the freezer for the dough to rest for at least 20 minutes.

Preheat the oven to 375°F (190°C). Bake one cookie at a time for 24 to 28 minutes, or until the edges are golden-brown. Allow it to cool down on the baking tray for about 20 minutes.

COCONUT + PASSION FRUIT PRESERVES VARIATION: For a tropical rendition of this recipe, substitute toasted coconut shreds for the mixed nuts and stuff it with passion fruit or mango preserves instead of peanut butter for a taste of the islands.

To toast the coconut shreds, preheat the oven to 325°F (163°C) and line a jelly roll pan with parchment paper. Spread out 1 cup (93 g) of coconut shreds evenly on the parchment paper and bake for 12 to 18 minutes, or until the edges of the shreds are a light brown color.

Follow the same instructions to make the cookie, but after adding in the vanilla extract, also add 3 tablespoons (45 ml) of coconut cream before incorporating the flour mixture. Then add the toasted coconut shreds.

When assembling the cookie, use your fingers or a spoon to create a small concave area on the center of the flattened dough circles that will be for the bottom of the cookie. Place ⅓ cup (80 ml) of passion fruit or mango preserve in the center of each. Make sure the top and bottom cookies are well sealed to avoid oozing preserves while baking. Top each cookie with ⅓ cup (44 g) of mixed nuts if desired. Follow the same baking and cooling instructions.

Banana Walnut Chocolate Chip

You know you have a sweet tooth if you love a pie or cake for breakfast. This cookie reminds me of banana cream pie, but better. The banana cream center adds a smooth and creamy contrast to the walnut cookie. The caramel sauce on top is like the cherry on top of a sundae—tying it all in together to make it one special treat!

Yield: 2 colossal cookies

Banana instant pudding mix (made with heavy cream)

1¾ cups (219 g) all-purpose flour

½ tsp baking powder

½ tsp baking soda

½ tsp salt

½ cup (114 g) unsalted butter, at room temperature

¾ cup (165 g) packed dark brown sugar

¼ cup (50 g) granulated white sugar

1 large egg, at room temperature

1 tsp pure vanilla extract

1 cup (240 g) mashed Roasted Bananas (page 183)

1¼ cups (146 g) chopped walnuts, divided

1 cup (170 g) chocolate chips, divided

4 tbsp (60 ml) Salted Caramel (page 177), or store bought

Make the banana pudding with heavy cream instead of milk. Whisk until the mixture thickens and the pudding comes together. I love the thicker texture of the pudding made with cream, and it works better for a cookie stuffing. Set the pudding in the refrigerator until needed for the cookie.

For the banana walnut cookie, whisk together the flour, baking powder, baking soda and salt and set aside.

Use the paddle attachment on a stand mixer to cream together the butter and brown and white sugar on medium speed for about 2 to 3 minutes until the mixture becomes fluffy and pale. Reduce the mixer speed to low and add in the egg, followed by the vanilla. Once these ingredients are well-incorporated, add in the bananas.

With the mixer speed on low, add in the flour mixture until the cookie dough just comes together. The dough will be stickier compared to other dough because of the roasted bananas, but it will all come together when baked.

Add in ¾ cup (88 g) of walnuts and ½ cup (85 g) of chocolate chips, and continue mixing for a few more seconds until they appear to be evenly distributed in the cookie dough.

Before starting with the cookie dough assembly, if you find the dough to be too sticky to work with, place the cookie dough in the refrigerator for 10 to 15 minutes.

To assemble the cookies, line a jelly roll pan with parchment paper and use this as your work area.

Roll ⅔ cup (160 ml) of cookie dough into a ball, and then use the palms of your hands to flatten it into a circle 5 inches (13 cm) in diameter. Repeat this step so you have 4 flattened cookie circles.

Use your fingers to gently press into the centers of 2 circles to create a concave area to hold the pudding. Use 3 tablespoons (45 ml) of banana pudding per cookie and place it in the concave area. Top with the other cookie circles. Use your fingers to pinch together the top and bottom edges of the cookie, and then smooth out the sides to create a seamless cookie.

Top the cookies with the remaining walnuts and chocolate chips. Press them gently onto the cookie dough to set in place. Place the tray with the cookies in the freezer for at least 20 minutes for the cookie dough to rest. Preheat the oven to 350°F (177°C).

Bake one cookie at a time for 24 to 28 minutes, or until the edges are golden-brown. Once the cookie is removed from the oven, allow it to cool on the baking tray for about 20 minutes before moving it to the cooling rack. If the cookie is moved too soon, it could break apart easily.

After the colossal cookies have completely cooled down, drizzle 2 tablespoons (30 ml) of caramel sauce (or more if you like!) over the top of each cookie!

Cranberry, Pistachio + Oatmeal

This is my version of a superfood cookie, or the closest that we will get to one here. Pistachios contain so many key nutrients, and I also added cranberries, which are rich in antioxidants and great for your heart. Enjoy this cookie for breakfast and take a mid-day cookie break for good health!

Yield: 2 colossal cookies

1 cup (125 g) all-purpose flour

½ tsp baking soda

½ tsp ground cinnamon

½ tsp salt

½ cup (114 g) unsalted butter, at room temperature

¾ cup (165 g) packed light brown sugar

2 tbsp (26 g) granulated white sugar

1 large egg, at room temperature

1 tsp pure vanilla extract

1⅓ cups (104 g) instant oatmeal

1 cup (121 g) dried cranberries, divided

1 cup (125 g) coarsely chopped pistachios, divided

7 tbsp (105 ml) cranberry preserves

Whisk together the flour, baking soda, cinnamon and salt and set aside.

Use the paddle attachment on a stand mixer to cream together the butter and brown and white sugar on medium speed for 2 to 3 minutes until the mixture is fluffy and pale. Reduce the mixer speed to low and add in the egg, followed by the vanilla.

With the mixer speed on low, add in the flour mixture. Once the cookie dough just comes together, add in the oatmeal, ¾ cup (91 g) of cranberries and ¾ cup (94 g) of pistachios. Continue to mix for a few more seconds to evenly distribute the ingredients.

To assemble the cookies, line a jelly roll pan with parchment paper and use this as your work area.

Roll ⅔ cup (160 g) of cookie dough into a ball, and then use the palms of your hands to flatten it into a 5-inch (13-cm) circle. Repeat this step so you have 4 flattened cookie circles.

Use your fingers to gently press into the center of 2 bottom cookies to create a small concave area to hold the preserves. Divide the cranberry preserves between the 2 cookies. Place the other flattened cookie dough on top and use your fingers to pinch together the top and bottom edges of the cookies, and then smooth out the sides for a seamless cookie.

Top the cookies with the remaining pistachios and cranberries and gently press them onto the cookie dough. Place the tray with the cookies in the freezer for the cookie dough to rest for at least 20 minutes. Preheat the oven to 375°F (190°C).

Bake one cookie at a time for 24 to 28 minutes, or until the edges are golden-brown. Once the cookie is removed from the oven, allow it to cool down on the baking tray for about 15 minutes before moving it to the cooling rack. It may break apart easily if moved too soon.

Peanut Butter, Pretzel + Chocolate Oatmeal

This cookie has a delicious sweet and savory contrast. The chocolate and caramel go so well together for sweetness, and the pretzel gives just the right about of saltiness. Though some may not see this as a breakfast cookie, I think the oatmeal helps to justify the "breakfast" part, or at least I'm always looking for a way to justify any cookie for breakfast. Even if you're not enjoying this for breakfast, it makes for a fantastic afternoon snack or a treat for a brunch potluck party!

Yield: 2 colossal cookies

1 cup (125 g) all-purpose flour

1 tsp baking soda

½ tsp baking powder

¼ tsp salt

½ cup (114 g) unsalted butter, at room temperature

¾ cup (165 g) packed dark brown sugar

¼ cup (50 g) granulated white sugar

1 large egg, at room temperature

1 tsp pure vanilla extract

½ cup (120 g) peanut butter

1⅓ cups (104 g) instant oatmeal

⅔ cup (113 g) plus ½ cup (85 g) chocolate chips, divided

⅔ cup plus ½ cup (70 g) roughly broken pretzels, divided

¼ cup (60 ml) Salted Caramel (page 177), or store bought

Whisk together the flour, baking soda, baking powder and salt and set aside.

Use the paddle attachment on a stand mixer to cream together the butter and brown and white sugar on medium speed for 2 to 3 minutes until the mixture is fluffy and light. Reduce the mixer speed to low and add in the egg. Once the egg is incorporated into the mixture, add the vanilla and peanut butter. Make sure the peanut butter is fully incorporated into the mixture before moving on to the next steps.

With the mixer speed on low, add in the flour mixture. Scrape the sides of the bowl as needed. Once the cookie dough just comes together, add in the oatmeal, ⅔ cup (113 g) of chocolate chips and ⅔ cup (40 g) of pretzels. Break the pretzels into quarters or halves, rather than a crumble of small pieces, because they will get crushed even more in the mixer. Allow the mixer to continue to mix for a few more seconds.

To assemble the cookies, line a jelly roll pan with parchment paper and use this as your work area.

Split the cookie dough in half. Roll each half into a ball, and then use the palm of your hands to flatten it into a circle 5 inches (13 cm) in diameter.

Mix together the remaining chocolate chips and pretzels and spread them all over each cookie and gently press them onto the dough to set them in place. Place the cookies in the freezer for at least 20 minutes for the dough to rest. Preheat the oven to 350°F (177°C).

Bake one cookie at a time for 22 to 26 minutes, or until the edges are golden-brown. After removing the cookie from the oven, allow it to cool down on the baking tray for about 10 minutes prior to moving it to the cooling rack. If the cookie is moved too soon, it may break apart.

After the cookie has completely cooled down, use a spoon to drizzle the caramel sauce over the cookie. Use as much caramel as you wish, but 2 tablespoons (30 ml) per cookie is recommended.

Oatmeal, Nuts + Toasted Coconut

Raspberry and coconut are a couple of my favorite things, and they complement each other so well. This breakfast cookie takes me to tropical daydreaming mode with the coconut cream incorporated into the dough and toasted coconut shreds in the cookie and on top. The crispy coconut shreds add the perfect texture to the oatmeal, nuts and raspberry preserve center. After one bite, you'll be daydreaming your way to the tropics as well!

Yield: 3 colossal cookies

1¼ cups (94 g) coconut shreds, divided

1 cup (125 g) all-purpose flour

½ tsp baking soda

½ tsp ground cinnamon

½ tsp salt

½ cup (114 g) unsalted butter, at room temperature

¾ cup (165 g) packed dark brown sugar

3 tbsp (39 g) granulated white sugar

1 large egg, at room temperature

1 tsp pure vanilla extract

3 tbsp (45 ml) coconut cream

1⅔ cups (134 g) instant oatmeal

½ cup (66 g) chopped nuts

9 tbsp (135 ml) raspberry preserves

For the coconut shreds, preheat the oven to 325°F (163°C) and line a jelly roll pan with parchment paper. Spread the shreds evenly on the parchment paper and bake for 12 to 18 minutes, or until the edges of the shreds are a light brown color.

For the oatmeal nut cookie, whisk together the flour, baking soda, cinnamon and salt and set aside.

Use the paddle attachment on a stand mixer to cream together the butter and brown and white sugar on medium speed for 2 to 3 minutes until the mixture becomes pale and fluffy. Reduce the mixer speed to low and add in the egg. Once the egg is incorporated into the mixture, add the vanilla and cream.

With the mixer speed on low, add in the flour mixture and continue to mix until the cookie dough just comes together. Add in the oatmeal, ½ cup (38 g) of coconut shreds and the nuts and continue to mix for a few seconds until they appear to be evenly distributed.

To assemble the cookies, line a jelly roll pan with parchment paper and use this as your work area.

Divide the dough into 6 equal parts. Roll each piece into a ball, and then use the palms of your hands to flatten each ball into a circle 4 inches (11 cm) in diameter.

Use your fingers to gently press into the center of 3 of the circles to create a small concave area to hold the raspberry preserve. Divide the raspberry preserves among the 3 dough circles. Top with the remaining flattened cookie circles. Use your fingers to pinch together the top and bottom edges of the cookie, and then smooth out the sides to create a seamless finish.

Top the cookies with the remaining toasted coconut shreds. Gently press the shreds on top of the cookie to ensure that they stay in place.

Place the tray of cookies in the freezer for at least 20 minutes for the cookie dough to rest. Preheat the oven to 350°F (177°C).

Bake one cookie at a time for 22 to 26 minutes, or until the edges are golden-brown. Allow the cookie to cool down on the baking tray for about 15 minutes before moving it to the cooling rack, otherwise it could break apart easily.

Browned Butter Oatmeal Cinnamon

This cookie reminds me of a pecan pie, but with a twist. The cherry preserves add a warm and fruity touch, and the browned butter enhances the nutty flavor, complementing the cinnamon spice and toasted pecans. I love a great pecan pie for breakfast, snack or for dessert. Or really this cookie.

Yield: 2 colossal cookies

¾ cup (82 g) coarsely chopped pecans

16 whole pecans

1 cup (125 g) all-purpose flour

1 tsp ground cinnamon

½ tsp baking soda

¼ tsp salt

½ cup (114 g) unsalted Browned Butter (page 183)

¾ cup (165 g) packed dark brown sugar

2 tbsp (26 g) granulated white sugar

1 large egg, at room temperature

1 tsp pure vanilla extract

1½ cups (120 g) instant oatmeal

6 tbsp (90 ml) cherry preserves

For the toasted pecans, preheat the oven to 325°F (163°C). Line a jelly roll pan with parchment paper and spread the chopped and whole pecans out on the pan. Bake for 5 to 8 minutes, but watch carefully after the 5-minute mark as they can burn easily.

For the cookie, whisk together the flour, cinnamon, baking soda and salt and set aside.

Use the paddle attachment on a stand mixer to combine the browned butter and brown and white sugar on medium speed for 3 to 4 minutes. The melted butter will make it more difficult to mix, so scrape down the sides occasionally, as the sugar and butter will stick to the sides of the bowl. Reduce the mixer speed to low and add in the egg, which will help the mixture become smoother. Once the egg is incorporated into the mixture, add the vanilla.

With the mixer speed on low, add in the flour mixture and continue to mix until the cookie dough just comes together. Add in the oatmeal and the chopped pecans, and mix for a few more seconds for them to distribute evenly in the cookie dough.

To assemble the cookies, line a jelly roll pan with parchment paper and use this as your work area.

Roll ⅔ cup (160 g) of cookie dough into a ball, and then use the palms of your hands to flatten it into a circle 5 inches (13 cm) in diameter. Repeat this step, so you will have 4 cookie circles.

Use your fingers to gently press into the centers of 2 of the circles to create a concave area to hold the preserves. Divide the preserves between the 2 cookies. Top with the other flattened cookie, covering the preserves. Use your fingers to pinch together the top and bottom edges of the cookie, and then smooth out the sides for a seamless finish.

Place 8 whole toasted pecans on top of each cookie and gently press each pecan onto the cookie dough to set it in place. Place the cookies in the freezer for the dough to rest for at least 20 minutes. Preheat the oven to 350°F (177°C).

Bake one cookie at a time for 24 to 28 minutes, or until edges are golden-brown. Once the cookie is removed from the oven, allow it to cool down on the baking tray for about 15 minutes, otherwise it may break apart easily if moved too soon to the cooling rack.

Year-Round Holiday Cookies

The best way to get yourself into the spirit for any holiday or occasion is to start baking a themed cookie! The following recipes are for my favorite occasions during the year, and of course, I need a cookie to celebrate each occasion. These are some of my most popular cookies, which makes them fun to share with others. I know, sometimes it's tough to share, but these are so exciting that your friends and family will love you even after enjoying these cookies!

Also, there's really no rule that says that you can't make a Valentine's cookie (page 133) on any other day than Valentine's. The Kick-Off (page 131) would be perfect for a football fanatic's birthday or a kid's sports team get together. To make it more fun, definitely look up when other countries celebrate holidays that are worthy of cookies. The possibilities are endless!

Candy Cane Surprise

Bring some Christmas cheer with a cookie stuffed with a candy cane sugar cookie. This festive cookie is decorated with peppermint candies to add a nice crunch. Break apart this chocolate cookie with the kids and watch their faces fill with excitement. They will start screaming with joy when they see the surprise stripes on the inside!

Yield: 2 colossal cookies

CHOCOLATE PEPPERMINT COOKIE

2⅔ cups (333 g) all-purpose flour

1⅓ cups (115 g) unsweetened cocoa powder

2 tsp (10 g) baking powder

1 tsp baking soda

1 tsp salt

1 cup (227 g) unsalted butter, at room temperature

⅔ cup (137 g) shortening, at room temperature

1⅓ cups (293 g) packed light brown sugar

½ cup (100 g) granulated white sugar

2 large eggs, at room temperature

2 tsp (10 ml) pure vanilla extract

1 tsp peppermint extract

CANDY CANE STRIPE SUGAR COOKIE

1⅓ cups (167 g) all-purpose flour

½ tsp baking soda

½ tsp cornstarch

¼ tsp salt

12 tbsp (170 g) unsalted butter, at room temperature

1 cup (200 g) granulated white sugar

1 large egg, at room temperature

1 tsp pure vanilla extract

2 tsp (10 ml) red food coloring

For the chocolate peppermint cookie, sift together the flour, cocoa, baking powder, baking soda and salt. Whisk together to ensure it is well combined and set aside.

Use the paddle attachment on a stand mixer to cream together the butter, shortening and brown and white sugar on medium speed for 2 to 3 minutes until the mixture becomes fluffy and pale. Reduce the mixer speed to low and add in one egg at a time, followed by the vanilla and peppermint, adding in each ingredient after the previous is fully incorporated into the mixture.

With the mixer speed on low, add in the flour mixture and continue to mix until the cookie dough just comes together. Wrap the dough in plastic wrap to prevent it from drying out.

For the candy cane stripe sugar cookie, whisk together the flour, baking soda, cornstarch and salt and set aside.

Use the paddle attachment on a stand mixer to cream together the butter and sugar on medium speed for 3 to 4 minutes until the mixture is fluffy and light. Reduce the mixer speed to low, and add in the egg. Once the egg is incorporated into the mixture, add the vanilla.

With the mixer speed on low, add in the flour mixture. Once the cookie dough just comes together, stop the mixer.

Divide the sugar cookie dough in half. Put half the cookie dough back in the mixer bowl and add the food coloring. Use the lowest speed to slowly incorporate the coloring. Once the color is evenly distributed, stop the mixer.

To assemble the cookies, line a jelly roll pan with parchment paper and use this as your work area.

Divide the chocolate peppermint cookie dough into 4 equal pieces. Roll each piece into a ball, and then use the palms of your hands to flatten each ball into a circle 5 inches (13 cm) in diameter.

Measure out ½ cup (80 g) of the white sugar cookie dough and ½ cup (80 g) of red sugar cookie dough. Roll each piece into a log 16 inches (41 cm) long and about ⅜ inch (1 cm) thick. Lay the 2 sugar cookie dough logs next to each other and gently curl the dough to create a red and white round swirl 5 inches (13 cm) in diameter. Repeat to form a second swirl.

Place the red and white swirls onto the centers of 2 flattened chocolate circles. Top with the other flattened chocolate circles. Use your fingers to pinch together the top and bottom edges of the cookie, and then smooth out the sides for a seamless finish.

(continued)

Candy Cane Surprise (Continued)

ADDITIONAL INGREDIENTS

⅔ cup (113 g) crushed peppermint candies or candy canes

½ cup (96 g) holiday sprinkles

⅔ cup (113 g) chocolate chips

Decorate the cookies by covering the entire surface area with crushed peppermint candies, sprinkles and chocolate chips. The easiest way I found to crush them was to place them into a small zip-lock bag and smash them with a wine bottle or olive oil bottle. Gently press them onto the cookie dough to set in place.

Place the tray of decorated cookies in the freezer for the cookie dough to rest for at least 20 minutes. Preheat the oven to 350°F (177°C).

Bake one cookie at a time for 30 to 35 minutes. One way to tell if the cookie is fully baked is if the center of the cookie does not have a dome shape, appears to have a light crust and does not appear to be raw dough. Once the cookie is removed from the oven, allow it to cool down on the baking tray for about 20 minutes prior to moving it to the cooling rack. Otherwise, you may risk the cookie breaking apart.

Sweet Greetings

A classic chocolate chip cookie might be what some people would like for the holidays, but the most exciting part about this cookie is the red and green sugar cookie surprise on the inside! For the holidays, we need to take it up a notch for a stuffed cookie and have not just one stuffed cookie inside, but TWO! So, even if the holidays are crazy busy—a double-stuffed cookie is definitely worth taking a moment to celebrate.

Yield: 2 colossal cookies

CHOCOLATE CHIP COOKIE
¾ cup (103 g) bread flour

½ cup (69 g) cake flour

½ tsp baking powder

½ tsp baking soda

¼ tsp salt

½ cup (114 g) unsalted butter, at room temperature

3 tbsp (39 g) shortening, at room temperature

¾ cup (165 g) packed dark brown sugar

½ cup (100 g) granulated white sugar

1 large egg, at room temperature

1 tsp pure vanilla extract

½ cup (85 g) chocolate chips

SUGAR COOKIE
1⅓ cups (167 g) all-purpose flour

½ tsp baking soda

½ tsp cornstarch

¼ tsp salt

½ cup plus 4 tbsp (170 g) unsalted butter, at room temperature

1 cup (200 g) granulated white sugar

1 large egg, at room temperature

1 tsp pure vanilla extract

2 tsp (10 ml) red gel food coloring

½ to 1 tsp green gel food coloring

For the chocolate chip cookie, whisk together the bread and cake flour, baking powder, baking soda and salt and set aside.

Use the paddle attachment on a stand mixer to cream together the butter, shortening and brown and white sugar on medium speed for 2 to 3 minutes until the mixture becomes fluffy and pale. Reduce the mixer speed to low, and add in the egg. Once the egg is incorporated into the mixture, add the vanilla.

With the mixer speed on low, add in the flour mixture and continue to mix until the cookie dough just comes together. Add in the chocolate chips and continue to mix for a few more seconds. Wrap the dough in plastic wrap to prevent it from drying out.

For the sugar cookie dough, whisk together the flour, baking soda, cornstarch and salt and set aside.

Use a paddle attachment on a stand mixer to cream together the butter and sugar on medium speed for 3 to 4 minutes until the mixture is fluffy and light. Reduce the mixer speed to low, and add in the egg. Once the egg is incorporated into the mixture, add the vanilla.

With the mixer speed on low, add in the flour mixture and allow the mixer to continue until the cookie dough just comes together.

Remove about one-third of the cookie dough from the bowl. Add the red food coloring to the dough still in the bowl. Mix on slow speed until the color is evenly distributed. Wash the bowl and repeat the steps for the green color with the remaining dough.

To assemble the cookies, line a jelly roll pan with parchment paper and use this as your work area.

Divide the chocolate chip cookie dough into 4 equal pieces. Roll each piece into a ball, and then use the palms of your hands to flatten each ball into a circle 5 inches (13 cm) in diameter.

Roll ¼ cup (60 g) of red sugar cookie dough into a ball, and then use the palms of your hands to flatten it into a circle 3½ inches (9 cm) in diameter. Repeat this step, so you will have 2 red sugar cookie circles. Place each one in the center of a chocolate chip circle.

Roll 3 tablespoons (45 g) of the green sugar cookie into a ball, and then use the palms of your hands to flatten it into a circle 2½ inches (6 cm) in diameter. Place the green sugar cookie in the center of one of the red sugar cookies and place the other chocolate chip with red sugar cookie face down over the green sugar cookie. The result is a green cookie inside a red cookie inside a chocolate chip cookie. Use your fingers to pinch together the top and bottom edges of the cookie, and smooth out the sides to create a seamless cookie.

Repeat the steps to make the second colossal cookie.

(continued)

Sweet Greetings (Continued)

ADDITIONAL INGREDIENTS
½ cup (96 g) holiday sprinkles
⅔ cups (113 g) chocolate chips

Let's decorate the cookies! I always start with the sprinkles because it's easier to press the sprinkles into the cookie dough without the chocolate chips in the way. Divide the sprinkles and chocolate chips between the cookies, and gently press them onto the dough to set them in place. Place the tray with the cookies in the freezer for the cookie dough to rest for at least 20 minutes. Preheat the oven to 350°F (177°C).

Bake one cookie at a time for 26 to 30 minutes, or until the edges are golden-brown. When the cookie is removed from the oven, allow it to cool down on the baking tray for about 20 minutes prior to moving it to the cooling rack. Since this is a larger colossal cookie, I recommend sliding the parchment paper or silicone baking mat with the cookie onto the cooling rack until it is fully cooled down.

Someone's Staring at You

Not sure what can be more spooky than a cookie with multiple eyes staring right back at you! Maybe oozy red velvet bleeding out from a chocolate chip cookie? Well, how about combining both together for a sweet and scary treat? Make Halloween just a little more thrilling with these cookies that will be loved by all ages!

Yield: 2 colossal cookies

CHOCOLATE CHIP COOKIE

1 cup (137 g) bread flour

1 cup (137 g) cake flour

¾ tsp baking powder

¾ tsp baking soda

¾ tsp salt

½ cup plus 3 tbsp (156 g) unsalted butter, at room temperature

¾ cup (165 g) packed dark brown sugar

¾ cup (150 g) granulated white sugar

1 large egg, at room temperature

1 tsp pure vanilla extract

2 tbsp (30 ml) heavy cream

½ cup (85 g) chocolate chips

RED VELVET COOKIE

1¾ cups (219 g) all-purpose flour

¼ cup (22g) unsweetened cocoa powder

½ tsp baking powder

½ tsp baking soda

¼ tsp salt

½ cup plus 2 tbsp (142 g) unsalted butter, at room temperature

¾ cup (165 g) packed dark brown sugar

¼ cup (50 g) granulated white sugar

1 large egg, at room temperature

1 tsp pure vanilla extract

2 tbsp (30 ml) heavy cream

2 tbsp (30 ml) red food coloring or gel coloring

For the chocolate chip cookie, whisk together the bread and cake flour, baking powder, baking soda and salt and set aside.

Use the paddle attachment on a stand mixer to cream together the butter and brown and white sugar on medium speed for 2 to 3 minutes until the mixture is fluffy and pale. Reduce the mixer speed to low and add in the egg. Once the egg is fully incorporated, add in the vanilla, followed by cream.

With the mixer speed on low, add in the flour mixture. Use a spatula to scrape the sides as needed to ensure all the ingredients are incorporated. Once the cookie dough just comes together, add in the chocolate chips. Wrap the cookie dough in plastic wrap to prevent it from drying out.

For the red velvet cookie, sift the flour, cocoa, baking powder, baking soda and salt together. Whisk to ensure all the ingredients are well combined and set aside.

Use the paddle attachment on a stand mixer to cream together the butter and brown and white sugar for about 2 to 3 minutes until the mixture is light and fluffy. Reduce the mixer speed to low and add in the egg. Once the egg is incorporated into the mixture, add the vanilla and cream. Add in the food coloring. I prefer to use gel food coloring because it will not thin out the batter as much as liquid food coloring.

Keep the mixer speed on low, and add in the flour mixture. Stop the mixer once the cookie dough just comes together. The red velvet cookie dough can be stickier due to the extra liquid from the food coloring, so if needed, place the cookie dough in the refrigerator for 10 to 15 minutes to make it easier to work with.

To assemble the cookies, line a jelly roll pan with parchment paper and use this as your work area.

Divide the chocolate chip cookie dough into 4 equal pieces. Roll each piece into a ball, and then use the palms of your hands to flatten each ball into a circle 5 inches (13 cm) in diameter.

Roll ⅓ cup (80 g) of the red velvet cookie dough into a ball, and then use the palms of your hands to flatten it into a circle 3 inches (8 cm) in diameter. Repeat, and place the red velvet circles in the center of the flattened chocolate chip cookie circles. Place the remaining chocolate chip cookie circles on top. Use your fingers to pinch together the top and bottom edges of the cookie, and then smooth out the sides for a seamless finish.

(continued)

Someone's Staring at You (Continued)

ADDITIONAL INGREDIENTS
⅔ cup (113 g) chocolate chips
Mini candy eyeballs

Cover each cookie with chocolate chips, and gently press them onto the cookie dough to set them in place. Place the tray with the cookies in the freezer for at least 20 minutes for the dough to rest before baking. Preheat the oven to 350°F (177°C).

Bake one cookie at a time for 22 to 25 minutes, or until the edges are golden-brown. Once the cookie is out of the oven, allow it to cool down on the baking tray for about 15 minutes before moving it to the cooling rack, otherwise it could break apart easily.

While you are waiting for the cookie to cool down, gently place and press the candy eyeballs onto the soft chocolate chips (be careful not to press too hard, otherwise the chocolate chip will get mushed in). The eyeballs need to go on after the cookie is baked because they melt in the oven. Add as many or as few eyes as you like, and it will most definitely make for a spooky Halloween cookie!

SPOOKY RED VELVET COOKIE VARIATION: For some extra fun with the excess red velvet cookie dough, make traditional-size cookies and cover them with a handful of chocolate chips. Bake at 350°F (177°C) for 12 to 15 minutes. After the cookie is removed from the oven, gently place and press candy eyeballs on each of the chocolate chips for some extra spooky fun!

Spooky Surprise

I always love the combination of chocolate and vanilla cookies, just like combining chocolate and vanilla ice cream together. This Halloween-themed cookie has a chocolatey exterior and fun surprise on the inside—a layer of orange sugar cookie plus sprinkles! If you use black sprinkles, it creates contrasting layers of black and orange when the cookie is broken open!

Yield: 4 colossal cookies

DOUBLE CHOCOLATE CHIP COOKIE

2 cups (250 g) all-purpose flour

⅔ cup (57 g) unsweetened cocoa powder

½ tsp baking powder

½ tsp baking soda

½ tsp salt

1 cup (227 g) unsalted butter, at room temperature

1½ cups (300 g) granulated white sugar

2 large eggs, at room temperature

2 tsp (10 ml) pure vanilla extract

3 tbsp (45 ml) heavy cream

¾ cup (128 g) chocolate chips

SUGAR COOKIE

2¼ cups (281 g) all-purpose flour

½ tsp baking powder

¼ tsp salt

1 cup (227 g) unsalted butter, at room temperature

1½ cups (300 g) granulated white sugar

1 large egg, at room temperature

½ tbsp (8 ml) pure vanilla extract

½ tsp orange gel or food coloring

1-2 drops red gel or food coloring

For the double chocolate chip cookies, sift together the flour, cocoa, baking powder, baking soda and salt. Whisk together to ensure everything is well combined and set aside.

Use the paddle attachment on a stand mixer to cream together the butter and sugar on medium speed for 3 to 4 minutes until the mixture is fluffy and light. Reduce the mixer speed to low and add in one egg at a time. Once the eggs are incorporated into the mixture, add the vanilla and cream.

With the mixer speed on low, add in the flour mixture and use a spatula to scrape down the sides as needed. Once the cookie dough just comes together, add in the chocolate chips and mix for a few more seconds. Wrap the dough in plastic wrap to prevent it from drying out.

For the sugar cookie dough, whisk together the flour, baking powder and salt and set aside.

Use the paddle attachment on a stand mixer to cream together the butter and sugar on medium speed for 3 to 4 minutes until the butter and sugar become fluffy and light. Reduce the mixer speed to low and add in the egg. Once the egg is incorporated into the mixture, add the vanilla.

With the mixer speed on low, add in the flour mixture and continue to mix until the cookie dough just comes together.

Since the sugar cookie recipe yields more dough than needed, remove about half of the dough. Mix the remaining dough with orange and red food coloring on low speed until the color is just combined. Add more coloring to reach the desired color, and note that a touch of red coloring gives the dough a more vibrant orange color.

To assemble the cookies, line a jelly roll pan with parchment paper and use this as your work area.

Divide the double chocolate chip cookie dough into 8 equal pieces. Roll each piece into a ball, and then use the palms of your hands to flatten each ball into a circle 4½ inches (11 cm) in diameter.

Roll ⅓ cup (80 g) of orange sugar cookie dough into a ball, and then use the palms of your hands to flatten it into a circle 3 inches (8 cm) in diameter. Repeat this seven more times. Place each of the flattened sugar circles onto the middle of a double chocolate chip circle.

(continued)

Spooky Surprise (Continued)

ADDITIONAL INGREDIENTS

1¼ cups (240 g) orange and black sprinkles

1 cup (170 g) chocolate chips

½ cup (85 g) mini candy pumpkins (optional)

Use a spoon or your fingers to press into the middle of four of the sugar cookies to create a concave area for the sprinkles. Make sure the concave area is not the entire surface area of the sugar cookie, but there's an edge all around. Then, scoop 3 tablespoons (36 g) of sprinkles into the concave area. Top with the remaining flattened cookies so you have sprinkles inside an orange sugar cookie inside a double chocolate cookie. Do your best to match up the orange cookie dough edges. Use your fingers to pinch together the top and bottom edges of the cookie, and then smooth out the sides for a seamless cookie.

Cover the cookies with the remaining sprinkles and press into place. Top with the chocolate chips and press into place.

Place the tray with the cookies in the freezer for at least 20 minutes to allow the cookie dough to rest. Preheat the oven to 350°F (177°C).

Bake the cookies one at a time for 24 to 28 minutes. After the cookie is removed from the oven, allow it to cool down on the baking tray for at least 15 minutes, since it could easily break apart if moved too soon.

As a finishing touch, gently press the candied pumpkins into the chocolate chips.

> NOTE: Candied pumpkins need to be added after baking, otherwise they would melt in the oven.

The Kick-Off

This football-shaped cookie will have everyone jumping with joy! Even though I can't tell you much about what is going on in the game or anything about the teams, I always love the Super Bowl. It's about the endless amount of food and gathering of people, so who really needs to know what's going on except for who's on the halftime show and what's at the dessert table? The chocolate cookie is fun and playful, and the best part is the chocolate chip cookie surprise.

Yield: 2 colossal football cookies

CHOCOLATE SUGAR COOKIE

2¼ cups (281 g) all-purpose flour

1 cup (86 g) unsweetened cocoa powder

¼ tsp salt

1 cup (227 g) unsalted butter, at room temperature

1 cup (200 g) granulated white sugar

½ cup (110 g) packed light brown sugar

2 large eggs, at room temperature

1 tsp pure vanilla extract

CHOCOLATE CHIP COOKIE

⅔ cup (92 g) bread flour

½ cup (69 g) cake flour

½ tsp baking powder

½ tsp baking soda

¼ tsp salt

½ cup plus 2 tbsp (142 g) unsalted butter, at room temperature

½ cup (110 g) packed dark brown sugar

½ cup (100 g) granulated white sugar

1 large egg, at room temperature

1 tsp pure vanilla extract

⅔ cup (113 g) mini chocolate chips

For the chocolate sugar cookie, sift together the flour, cocoa and salt. Whisk to ensure everything is well combined and set aside.

Use the paddle attachment on a stand mixer to cream together the butter and white and brown sugar on medium speed for 2 to 3 minutes until the mixture is light and fluffy. Reduce the mixer speed to low and add in the eggs one at a time. Once the egg is incorporated into the mixture, add the vanilla.

With the mixer speed on low, add in the flour mixture and scrape the sides of the bowl as needed. Once the dough just comes together, stop the mixer. Wrap the dough in plastic wrap to prevent it from drying out.

For the chocolate chip cookie, whisk together the bread and cake flour, baking powder, baking soda and salt and set aside.

Use the paddle attachment on a stand mixer to cream together the butter and brown and white sugar on medium speed for 2 to 3 minutes until the mixture is pale and fluffy. Reduce the mixer speed to low, and add in the egg. Once the egg is incorporated into the mixture, add the vanilla.

With the mixer speed on low, add in the flour mixture. When the dough just comes together, add in the mini chocolate chips, and mix for a few more seconds.

To assemble the cookies, line a jelly roll pan with parchment paper and use this as your work area.

Roll 1 cup (240 g) of chocolate sugar cookie dough into a ball, and use your hands to flatten and mold the dough into the shape of a football about 9½ inches (24 cm) long and 4½ inches (11 cm) wide. After shaping the dough, use your fingers to create a small edge around the perimeter of the football.

Fill inside the perimeter of the football with ½ cup (120 g) of chocolate chip cookie dough, and keep it within the chocolate sugar cookie dough edge. Use more chocolate chip cookie dough if needed to fill in the center.

Flatten 1 cup (240 g) of chocolate sugar cookie dough into the shape and size of the football you've already created for the base. Place over the chocolate chip layer and shape to fit the base of the football. Join the top and bottom edges of the cookie together. Use your fingers to smooth out the edges to create a seamless finish.

Repeat the above steps for the second colossal football cookie. Place the tray with the cookies in the freezer for the cookie dough to rest for at least 30 minutes. Preheat the oven to 350°F (177°C).

(continued)

The Kick-Off (Continued)

1 cup (240 ml) Vanilla Buttercream
(page 182)

Bake the football cookies one at a time for 30 to 35 minutes. Since it can be difficult to gauge if it's fully baked, check to see if the center of the football is still doughy. If not then the cookie is done. If it is still wet, check back on the cookie at 3-minute intervals. If the edges are starting to crack a little bit, then you know that the cookie is either done or about ready.

Allow the cookie to cool down on the baking tray for at least 20 to 30 minutes. Due to the size of the football cookie, it takes a while for it to cool down. I recommend sliding the cookie with the parchment paper or silicone baking mat to the cooling rack rather than attempting to move the cookie. Once the cookie is on the cooling rack you can place the tray in the refrigerator for 10 to 15 minutes if you're in a hurry. The cookie cannot be decorated until it's fully cooled down, otherwise, you'll end up with messy buttercream laces dripping along the side of your football!

To pipe the buttercream, use an open round piping tip (Wilton 12) for a more prominent lace. If you only have a thin round tip, then I would recommend piping more lines together to make it look like one thick line.

Only for My Sweetheart

If your Valentine is a chocolate chip cookie lover, this could be just the cookie for them! I love that this chocolate chip cookie is stuffed with red velvet cookie AND white chocolate ganache. The red velvet has an irresistibly soft texture and decadent flavor that contrasts perfectly with the lightly crisped chocolate chip exterior. The white chocolate ganache adds the perfect sweet touch. Make this for your Valentine and they will feel lucky that they have someone as fabulous as you!

Yield: 4 colossal cookies

CHOCOLATE CHIP COOKIE

2½ cups (281 g) all-purpose flour

2 tsp (10 g) baking powder

½ tsp salt

1 cup (227 g) unsalted butter, at room temperature

1½ cups (330 g) packed light brown sugar

½ cup (100 g) granulated white sugar

2 large eggs, at room temperature

2 tsp (10 ml) pure vanilla extract

½ cup (85 g) dark chocolate chips

½ cup (85 g) white chocolate chips

RED VELVET COOKIE

1½ cups (188 g) all-purpose flour

¼ cup (22 g) unsweetened cocoa powder

½ tsp baking powder

½ tsp baking soda

¼ tsp salt

½ cup plus 2 tbsp (142 g) unsalted butter, at room temperature

½ cup (110 g) packed light brown sugar

½ cup (100 g) granulated white sugar

1 large egg, at room temperature

1 tsp pure vanilla extract

2 tbsp (30 ml) heavy cream

2 tbsp (30 ml) red food coloring or gel coloring

For the chocolate chip cookie, whisk together the flour, baking powder and salt and set aside.

Use the paddle attachment on a stand mixer to cream together the butter and brown and white sugar on medium speed for about 2 to 3 minutes until the mixture is fluffy and pale. Reduce the mixer speed to low, and add in the eggs one at a time. Once the eggs are incorporated into the mixture, add the vanilla.

With the mixer speed on low, add in the flour mixture and continue to mix until the cookie dough just comes together. Add in both the dark and white chocolate chips and continue to mix for a few more seconds. Wrap the cookie dough in plastic wrap to prevent the dough from drying out.

For the red velvet cookie, sift the flour, cocoa, baking powder, baking soda and salt together. Whisk to make sure they are well-combined and set aside.

Use the paddle attachment on a stand mixer to cream together the butter with the brown and white sugar for 2 to 3 minutes until the mixture is pale and fluffy. Once combined, reduce the mixer speed to low and add the egg. Once the egg is incorporated, add in the vanilla, followed by the cream and food coloring. I prefer to use gel food coloring, because it will not thin out the batter as much as liquid food coloring.

With the mixer speed on low, add in the flour mixture and stop the mixer once the cookie dough just comes together. If you find that the red velvet cookie dough is too sticky—which could happen if using liquid food coloring—place the cookie dough in the refrigerator for about 10 to 15 minutes to make it easier to work with.

To assemble the cookies, line a jelly roll pan with parchment paper and use this as your work area.

Divide the chocolate chip cookie dough into 8 equal pieces. Roll each piece into a ball, and then use the palms of your hands to flatten each ball into a circle 5 inches (13 cm) in diameter.

Roll 3 tablespoons (45 g) of red velvet cookie dough into a ball, and then use the palms of your hands to flatten it into a circle 3 inches (8 cm) in diameter. Repeat this step until you have 8 flattened red velvet cookie circles. Place the red velvet circles in the center of the chocolate chip circles.

(continued)

Only for My Sweetheart (Continued)

ADDITIONAL INGREDIENTS

6 tbsp (90 ml) White Chocolate
Ganache (page 178), or store-bought

½ cup (96 g) Valentine-themed sprinkles

1 cup (170 g) chocolate chips

Use your fingers to gently press into the center of the 4 of the red velvet circles to create a small concave area to hold the ganache. Scoop 1½ tablespoons (22 ml) of ganache into the center of the concave cookie circles. Place the other flattened cookie dough on top and try to align the red velvet edges together. This does not need to be perfect, but matching it together creates a stronger seal for the ganache between the red velvet cookies. Use your fingers to pinch together the top and bottom edges of the chocolate cookie, and then smooth out the sides for a seamless finish.

Sprinkle Valentine's sprinkles all over each cookie, and use your fingers to gently press them onto the cookie dough to set them in place. Sprinkle chocolate chips on top of each cookie and gently press them onto the cookie dough. Place the tray with the cookies in the freezer and allow them to rest for at least 20 minutes. Preheat the oven to 350°F (177°C).

Bake one cookie at a time for 24 to 28 minutes, or until the edges are golden-brown. Allow the cookie to cool down on the baking tray before moving it to the cooling rack. If the cookie is moved too soon, it could break apart easily.

Sprinkle Some Love

This is a romantic cookie version of strawberries dipped in chocolate! What makes the strawberry sugar cookie so incredible is that the strawberry flavor is from freeze-dried strawberry powder infused with sugar, so you will have a natural touch of strawberry in the center of your cookie! Nothing says, "I love you" better than a chocolate cookie stuffed with a sweet strawberry cookie!

Yield: 2 colossal cookies

DOUBLE CHOCOLATE CHIP COOKIE

1¼ cups (156 g) all-purpose flour

¾ cup (38 g) chocolate fudge instant pudding mix

¼ cup (22 g) unsweetened cocoa powder

1 tsp baking soda

¼ tsp salt

½ cup (114 g) unsalted butter, at room temperature

½ cup (110 g) packed dark brown sugar

½ cup (100 g) granulated white sugar

1 large egg, at room temperature

1 tsp pure vanilla extract

2 tbsp (30 ml) heavy cream

½ cup (85 g) chocolate chips

STRAWBERRY SUGAR COOKIE

1 cup plus 1 tbsp (134 g) all-purpose flour

½ tsp baking soda

¼ tsp salt

¾ cup (150 g) granulated white sugar

1 cup (20 g) freeze-dried strawberries

½ cup plus 2 tbsp (142 g) unsalted butter, at room temperature

1 large egg, at room temperature

1 tsp pure vanilla extract

¼ tsp red gel food coloring (optional)

ADDITIONAL INGREDIENTS

¼ cup (48 g) Valentine-themed sprinkles

½ cup (85 g) chocolate chips

For the double chocolate chip cookie, sift together the flour, pudding mix, cocoa, baking soda and salt. Whisk together the ingredients to ensure they are well combined and set aside.

Use the paddle attachment on a stand mixer to cream together the butter and brown and white sugar on medium speed for 2 to 3 minutes until the mixture is pale and fluffy. Reduce the mixer speed to low and add in the egg. Once the egg is incorporated into the mixture, add the vanilla and the cream. With the mixer speed on low, add in the flour mixture and continue to mix until the cookie dough just comes together. Add in the chocolate chips and allow the mixer to continue for a few more seconds. Wrap the cookie dough in plastic wrap to prevent it from drying out.

For the strawberry sugar cookie, whisk together the flour, baking soda and salt and set aside.

To make strawberry sugar, use a food processor to pulse the sugar and freeze-dried strawberries together until powdered. Use the paddle attachment on a stand mixer to cream together the butter and strawberry sugar on medium speed. The strawberry sugar is fragrant, so you'll have the pleasure of enjoying the sweet scent of strawberries in the air as the mixer is creaming the butter and sugar together. After 3 to 4 minutes, the mixture will become fluffy and pale pink. Reduce the mixer speed to low and add in the egg. Once the egg is incorporated into the mixture, add the vanilla.

Continuing with the mixer speed on low, add in the flour mixture and mix until the cookie dough just comes together. At this point, the cookie dough will be a beautiful light pink color. After it is baked, it will be a light pink-brown color. If you would like a stronger pink or red color, I recommend adding a few drops of food coloring until the desired color is achieved.

To assemble the cookies, line a jelly roll pan with parchment paper and use this as your work area. Divide the chocolate cookie dough into 4 pieces. Roll each piece into a ball, and then flatten them with the palms of your hands into a circle 5 inches (13 cm) in diameter. Roll ⅓ cup (80 g) of strawberry sugar cookie dough into a ball, and then use the palms of your hands to flatten it into a circle 3 inches (8 cm) in diameter. Place the flattened sugar cookie dough in the middle of one of the flattened chocolate cookie circles. Place the other flattened chocolate cookie on top of the strawberry sugar cookie. Use your fingers to pinch together the top and bottom edges of the cookie, and then smooth out the sides for a seamless cookie. Repeat for the second colossal cookie.

Top the cookies with Valentine's sprinkles and chocolate chips. Gently press the toppings onto the cookie dough to set them in place. Place the tray with the cookies in the freezer for the cookie dough to rest for at least 20 minutes before baking. Preheat the oven to 350°F (177°C).

Bake one cookie at a time for 24 to 28 minutes. Allow it to cool down for about 15 minutes prior to moving it to the cooling rack.

Red, White + Blue Striped Surprise

There is no better way to celebrate the 4th of July than a chocolate chip cookie with a red, white and blue sugar cookie surprise on the inside! The fun and vibrant colors of our nation's flag make this a treat that everyone will love to break open to see. Another great part is that it's easy to change the surprise colors to celebrate any holiday!

Yield: 4 colossal cookies

CHOCOLATE CHIP COOKIE

2½ cups (281 g) all-purpose flour

⅔ cup (92 g) bread flour

1½ tsp (8 g) baking soda

½ tsp salt

1 cup plus 4 tbsp (283 g) unsalted butter, at room temperature

1½ cups (330 g) packed dark brown sugar

½ cup (100 g) granulated white sugar

2 large eggs, at room temperature

2 tsp (10 g) pure vanilla extract

SUGAR COOKIE

2¼ cups (281 g) all-purpose flour

½ tsp baking powder

¼ tsp salt

1 cup (227 g) unsalted butter, at room temperature

1½ cups (300 g) granulated white sugar

1 large egg, at room temperature

½ tbsp (8 ml) pure vanilla extract

1 tsp red gel food coloring

¼ tsp blue food coloring

ADDITIONAL INGREDIENTS

1 cup (192 g) red, white and blue sprinkles

1 cup (170 g) chocolate chips

For the chocolate chip cookie, whisk together the all-purpose and bread flour, baking soda and salt and set aside.

Use the paddle attachment on a stand mixer to cream together the butter and brown and white sugar for 2 to 3 minutes until the mixture is fluffy and pale. Reduce the mixer speed to low, and add in one egg at a time. Once the eggs are incorporated into the mixture, add the vanilla. With the mixer speed on low, add in the flour mixture and continue to mix until the cookie dough just comes together. Wrap the cookie dough in plastic wrap to prevent it from drying out. Keep in mind that we're holding the chocolate chips until the end.

For the sugar cookie, whisk together the flour, baking powder and salt and set aside.

Use the paddle attachment on a stand mixer to cream together the butter and sugar on medium speed for 3 to 4 minutes until the mixture becomes fluffy and pale. Reduce the mixer speed to low and add in the egg. Once the egg is incorporated into the mixture, add the vanilla. With the mixer speed on low, add in the flour mixture and continue to mix until the cookie dough just comes together. Remove the cookie dough from the mixer and split the sugar cookie into 3 equal pieces.

The recommended amount of food coloring will yield a saturated color tone, but add the amount that achieves the shade of red or blue you like. Place one cookie dough piece into the mixer and mix it on the slowest speed with the red food coloring, until the color is evenly distributed, but do not overmix. Clean the bowl and repeat for the blue. The third piece remains uncolored.

To assemble the cookies, line a jelly roll pan with parchment paper and use this as your work area. Split each color of sugar cookie dough in half. Roll each piece into a log 12 inches (30 cm) in length. Line the 3 different colored logs next to each other and cut them into 4 equal sections of tri-colored cookie dough. Roll each section into a ball, and then use the palms of your hands to flatten it into a circle 3 inches (8 cm) in diameter. Make sure that the side to be flattened has all 3 colors as evenly distributed as possible. Set the flattened cookie circles to the side.

Divide the chocolate chip cookie dough into 8 equal pieces. Roll each piece into a ball, and use the palms of your hands to flatten each ball into a circle 5 inches (13 cm) in diameter. Place a red, white and blue circle in the middle of 4 of the chocolate chip cookie circles. Top with the remaining chocolate chip cookie circles. Use your fingers to pinch together the top and bottom edges of the cookie, and then smooth out the sides for a seamless cookie.

Cover the top of each cookie with sprinkles all over, gently pressing them onto the dough to set them in place. Repeat with the chocolate chips and press into place.

Place the tray of cookies in the freezer for at least 20 minutes to allow the cookie dough to rest. Preheat the oven to 350°F (177°C). Bake one cookie at a time for 24 to 28 minutes. Allow it to cool down on the baking tray for about 15 minutes before moving it to the cooling rack.

Colossal Easter Egg Hunt

I love the sensation of breaking open this Easter egg cookie! This is the grown-up version of those little Easter eggs filled with chocolate. But this Easter egg sugar cookie is filled with dark and white chocolate stripes of delicious ganache! This cookie makes me feels like a kid again, especially with all the fun that I have using bright and colorful sprinkles to decorate it! Easter will never been the same without a colossal egg cookie!

Yield: 2 colossal cookies

3 cups (375 g) all-purpose flour

1 tsp baking powder

½ tsp salt

1 cup (227 g) unsalted butter, at room temperature

1 cup (200 g) granulated white sugar

2 large eggs, at room temperature

½ tbsp (8 ml) pure vanilla extract

2 tbsp (30 ml) heavy cream

7 tbsp (105 ml) Dark Chocolate Ganache (page 178), or store-bought, refrigerated

8 tbsp (120 ml) White Chocolate Ganache (page 178), or store-bought, refrigerated

1 cup (192 g) various colored sprinkles

For the sugar cookie, whisk together the flour, baking powder and salt and set aside.

Use the paddle attachment on a stand mixer to cream together the butter and sugar on medium speed for 3 to 4 minutes until the mixture is fluffy and pale. Reduce the mixer speed to low and add in one egg at a time. Once the eggs are incorporated into the mixture, add the vanilla and the cream.

With the mixer speed on low, add in the flour mixture and stop the mixer once the cookie dough just comes together.

To assemble the cookies, line a jelly roll pan with parchment paper and use this as your work area.

Divide the dough into 4 equal pieces. Roll each piece into a ball, and then flatten it on the parchment paper into an egg shape 6½ inches (17 cm) high and 5 inches (13 cm) wide. Form a small edge around the perimeter of 2 egg shapes to hold the ganache in place.

To fill the inside of the eggs, we will create four alternating horizontal stripes of ganache going across the egg. Since the ganache has been in the refrigerator, it should be more solid, which makes it easier to control the placement inside the egg. If the ganache is still too viscose or becomes too soft while working with it, place the ganache back in the refrigerator for about 5 minutes. Spread 1½ tablespoons (22 ml) of dark chocolate ganache inside the top quarter of the egg. Spread 2 tablespoons (30 ml) of white chocolate ganache below the dark chocolate for the next stripe. Spread another 2 tablespoons (30 ml) of dark chocolate ganache and another 2 tablespoons (30 ml) of white chocolate ganache at the bottom of the egg. If the ganache becomes too soft, place the tray with the cookie into the refrigerator for about 5 to 10 minutes for the ganache to harden. This will make it easier to work with for the next step.

Cover the ganache with the remaining egg-shaped dough. This is when having the hardened ganache helps, because you will need to press the top layer a little bit to cover the entire surface area of the egg. If the ganache is too soft, it could spill out of the egg. With the top layer fully covering the bottom, gently smooth the dough along the outer edges for a seamless egg. This step is important because the ganache will turn to liquid chocolate while baking and could leak out.

Decorate the entire surface area of each egg with sprinkles. I had a great time decorating my Easter egg cookie by using different colored sprinkles to create a striped design! Gently press the sprinkles into the cookie dough to set them in place. Place the tray with the cookies in the freezer for at least 30 minutes for the dough to rest. Preheat the oven to 350°F (177°C).

Bake one cookie at a time for 30 to 35 minutes, or until the edges are golden-brown. Allow the cookie to cool down on the baking tray for about 30 minutes prior to moving it to the cooling rack. I recommend sliding the parchment paper or silicone baking mat with the cookie to the cooling tray. The initial cooling period is especially important for the Easter egg, because the ganache is in a liquid state from being in the oven, making the cookie even more fragile.

Summer Tie-Dye

If you're going to a BBQ, definitely bring these tie-dye cookies. They will stand out among the crowd of foods and desserts! The red, white and blue tie-dye swirl makes this sugar cookie so much fun for everyone, and it has a chocolate cookie surprise in the middle! This is the perfect sweet treat after all those burgers and hot dogs, and is the best end to the evening!

Yield: 4 colossal cookies

TIE-DYE SUGAR COOKIE

4½ cups (563 g) all-purpose flour

1 tsp baking powder

½ tsp salt

2 cups (454 g) unsalted butter, at room temperature

3 cups (600 g) granulated white sugar

2 large eggs, at room temperature

1 tbsp (15 ml) pure vanilla extract

2 tsp (10 ml) red gel food coloring

½ tsp blue food coloring

CHOCOLATE SUGAR COOKIE

1 cup plus 2 tbsp (142 g) all-purpose flour

½ cup (43 g) unsweetened cocoa powder

¼ tsp salt

½ cup (114 g) unsalted butter, at room temperature

½ cup (100 g) granulated white sugar

¼ cup (55 g) packed light brown sugar

1 large egg, at room temperature

1 tsp pure vanilla extract

For the tie-dye sugar cookie, whisk together the flour, baking powder and salt and set aside.

Use the paddle attachment on a stand mixer to cream together the butter and sugar on medium speed for 3 to 4 minutes until fluffy and pale. Reduce the mixer speed to low and add in one egg at a time. Once the eggs are incorporated into the mixture, add the vanilla. Keep the mixer speed on low and add in the flour mixture. Stop the mixer once the cookie dough just comes together. Remove the cookie dough from the mixer and split it into 3 equal parts.

The recommended amount of food coloring yields a saturated color tone, but the amount to be used also depends on the shade of red or blue you would like to achieve. Place one piece of the cookie dough into the mixer, add the red coloring and mix on the slowest speed until the color is evenly distributed, but do not overmix. Clean the bowl and paddle and repeat for the blue color. Wrap each cookie dough color individually in plastic wrap to keep it from drying out.

For the chocolate sugar cookie, sift together the flour, cocoa and salt. Whisk together to ensure everything is well combined and set aside.

Use the paddle attachment on a stand mixer to cream together the butter and white and brown sugar on medium speed for 2 to 3 minutes until the mixture is pale and fluffy. Reduce the mixer speed to low and add in the egg, followed by the vanilla. With the mixer speed on low, add in the flour mixture and continue to mix until the cookie dough just comes together.

To assemble the cookies, line a jelly roll pan with parchment paper and use this as your work area. Split each piece of colored sugar cookie dough in half, and then roll each piece into logs that are 12 inches (30 cm) in length. Line up the 3 different colored logs next to each other and roll them together into one strip. Start from one end and twist the cookie dough so the colors become intertwined. Don't worry if a section breaks off—if so, push the cookie dough sections back together. The more twists, the tighter the color strips in the tie-dye will be. Cut the long twisted strips in half and roll each half into a ball. The colors should be incorporated together similar to tie-dye. Use the palms of your hands to flatten each ball into a circle 5 inches (13 cm) in diameter. You should have 8 tie-dye circles.

Roll ¼ cup (60 g) of chocolate cookie dough into a ball, and then use the palms of your hands to flatten it into a circle 3 inches (8 cm) in diameter. Repeat 3 times. Set a flattened chocolate circle in the center of one of the tie-dyed sugar cookies. Top with another sugar cookie circle, and then use your fingers to pinch together the top and bottom edges of the sugar cookie, and then smooth out the sides for a seamless finish. Repeat for the remaining cookies.

Place the cookies in the freezer for at least 20 minutes for the dough to rest. Preheat the oven to 350°F (177°C).

Bake one cookie at a time for 24 to 28 minutes, or until the edges are light golden-brown. Allow it to cool down on the baking tray for about 15 minutes prior to moving it to the cooling rack.

Eat Sweets and Be Thankful

I love this recipe because it reminds me of a warm pumpkin pie with marshmallows on top, but this is a million times better because nothing beats a soft pumpkin cookie filled with a gooey marshmallow surprise! Heat it up and eat it warm for melt-in-your-mouth greatness!

Yield: 3 colossal cookies

¾ cup (180 ml) pumpkin puree

2¼ cups (281 g) all-purpose flour

1 tsp baking powder

1 tsp baking soda

1 tsp ground cinnamon

½ tsp salt

1 cup (227 g) unsalted Browned Butter (page 183)

¾ cup (165 g) packed light brown sugar

¼ cup (50 g) granulated white sugar

1 large egg, at room temperature

1 tsp pumpkin pie spice extract

1 tsp pure vanilla extract

2 tbsp (30 ml) maple syrup

¾ cup (180 ml) marshmallow fluff

3 tbsp (21 g) pumpkin seeds

6 tbsp (64 g) dark chocolate chips

6 tbsp (64 g) white chocolate chips

Remove the moisture from the pumpkin puree by wrapping it in a few paper towels and squeezing out the water over the sink. This step is important for the cookie to have a crisper, versus cakey, texture. Remove from the towels and set aside.

For the pumpkin cookie, whisk together the flour, baking powder, baking soda, cinnamon and salt and set aside.

Use the paddle attachment on a stand mixer to mix the browned butter and brown and white sugar together on low speed until the mixture is smooth. Add in the egg, followed by the pumpkin pie spice extract, vanilla and maple syrup, adding in each ingredient after the previous one is fully incorporated. With the mixer speed on low, add in the pumpkin puree, and then the flour mixture. Once the cookie dough just comes together, stop the mixer.

To assemble the cookies, line a jelly roll pan with parchment paper and use this as your work area.

Divide the cookie dough into 6 equal pieces. Roll each piece into a ball, and then use the palms of your hands to flatten each ball into a circle 5 inches (13 cm) in diameter. Divide the fluff among 3 circles, and top with another cookie circle. (You can use ⅓ cup [15 g] of mini marshmallows for each cookie instead of fluff.) Use your fingers to pinch together the top and bottom edges of the cookie and smooth out the sides for a seamless finish.

Decorate the cookies with pumpkin seeds and white and dark chocolate chips. Gently press them onto the cookie dough to set in place.

Place the tray with the cookies in the freezer for the cookie dough to rest for at least 20 minutes. Preheat the oven for 350°F (177°C).

Bake one cookie at a time for 22 to 26 minutes, or until the edges are golden-brown. Allow it to cool down on the baking sheet for about 15 minutes before moving it to the cooling rack or it could break apart easily.

Ringing in the New Year

The black and white color combination makes this the appropriate black-tie cookie for any New Year's celebration. The salted caramel center adds the right amount of heavenly sweetness everyone needs to ensure the New Year is off to a sweet start! The most important part of this cookie could be that there is espresso powder incorporated into the chocolate cookie. This key pick-me-up will keep you wide awake for the countdown to midnight so you can dance right into the New Year!

Yield: 2 colossal cookies

SUGAR COOKIE

1¼ cups (156 g) all-purpose flour

¼ cup (13 g) vanilla instant pudding mix

½ tsp baking soda

¼ tsp salt

7 tbsp (98 g) unsalted butter, at room temperature

2 tbsp (26 g) shortening, at room temperature

½ cup (110 g) packed light brown sugar

½ cup (100 g) granulated white sugar

1 large egg, at room temperature

1 tsp pure vanilla extract

½ cup (85 g) dark chocolate chips

½ cup (85 g) white chocolate chips

CHOCOLATE-ESPRESSO COOKIE

1 cup (125 g) all-purpose flour

¼ cup (22 g) unsweetened cocoa powder

1 tsp espresso powder

½ tsp baking soda

⅛ tsp salt

½ cup plus 2 tbsp (142 g) unsalted butter, at room temperature

¾ cup (150 g) granulated white sugar

1 large egg, at room temperature

1 tsp pure vanilla extract

2 tbsp (30 ml) heavy cream

ADDITIONAL INGREDIENTS

¼ cup (60 ml) Salted Caramel (page 177)

¼ cup (48 g) festive sprinkles

¼ cup (43 g) dark chocolate chips

¼ cup (43 g) white chocolate chips

For the sugar cookie, whisk together the flour, pudding mix, baking soda and salt and set aside.

Use the paddle attachment on a stand mixer to cream the butter, shortening and brown and white sugar together on medium speed for 3 to 4 minutes until the mixture is fluffy and pale. Reduce the mixer speed to low and add in the egg. Once the egg is incorporated into the mixture, add the vanilla. With the mixer speed on low, add in the flour mixture and continue to mix until the cookie dough just comes together. Scrape the sides of the bowl as needed. Add in the dark and white chocolate chips and continue to mix for a few more seconds. Wrap the cookie dough in plastic wrap to prevent it from drying out.

For the chocolate-espresso cookie, sift together the flour, cocoa, espresso, baking soda and salt. Whisk the ingredients to ensure they are well combined and set aside.

Use the paddle attachment on a stand mixer to cream together the butter and sugar on medium speed for 3 to 4 minutes until the mixture becomes fluffy and pale. Reduce the mixer speed to low and add in the egg. Once the egg is incorporated into the mixture, add the vanilla and the cream.

With the mixer speed on low, add in the flour mixture and continue to mix until the cookie dough just comes together.

To assemble the cookies, line a jelly roll pan with parchment paper and use this as your work area. Divide the sugar cookie dough into 4 equal pieces. Roll each piece into a ball, and then use the palms of your hands to flatten each ball into a circle 5 inches (13 cm) in diameter. Roll ⅓ cup (80 g) of chocolate-espresso cookie dough into a ball, and then use the palms of your hands to flatten it into a circle 3 inches (8 cm) in diameter. Place the chocolate circle onto one of the sugar cookie circles. Use your fingers to create a small concave area within the chocolate cookie to hold the caramel. Scoop 2 tablespoons (30 ml) of caramel into the concave area. Top with another flattened sugar cookie circle. Use your fingers to pinch together the top and bottom edges of the cookie, and then smooth out the sides to create a seamless cookie. Repeat to make a second cookie.

Cover both cookies with sprinkles—I love black and white sprinkles to keep with the New Year's theme. Press the sprinkles into the cookie. Mix together the white and dark chocolate chips in a small bowl. Spread the chips over the cookies and gently press into place.

Place the tray with the cookies in the freezer for at least 20 minutes for the cookie dough to rest. Preheat the oven to 350°F (177°C).

Bake one cookie at a time for 24 to 28 minutes, or until the edges are light golden-brown. Allow the cookie to cool on the baking tray for about 20 minutes before sliding the silicone mat or parchment paper onto the cooling rack.

Shortcut Cookies: Assemble and Bake It

No one has to know that we took a shortcut. There is nothing better than a homemade cookie from scratch, but sometimes I just need a shortcut. When you're just too busy or want to take longer than a moment to sit and binge-watch some more television, this is the best back-up plan. Pretend you spent some quality effort in making these cookies—it will be our little secret, and I promise not to tell as long as you don't either.

These recipes cover two convenient options for easy homemade colossal cookies: cookie mix, which is dry in a bag; and pre-made dough, which is easily found in the refrigerated section of any grocery store. Cookie mix is easier to customize. You can add more ingredients to make it a distinctly different colossal cookie. Follow the packaging instructions, whether it be by adding eggs, oil or butter, and then I will give you the tips on how to make it that much better. It's easy and there are so many great possibilities to add a twist and create that WOW factor.

Some recipes use pre-made dough, so you don't even need a mixer. All you need are a few extra ingredients. Once the cookie is baked, you get to be the superstar with fantastic colossal cookies to rave about. It doesn't have to be tough to be fabulous, and I'm excited to show you how easy it really is!

One quick note about cookie mixes and pre-made dough: I've found that they tend to spread out more when baking and result in a flatter cookie.

Chocolate Chip + Sugar Cookie

I love chocolate chip cookies, and when combined with a touch of sugar cookie in the middle, they are even better. But what makes this cookie phenomenal? Sprinkles on the inside! The additional ingredients needed are minimal, and this is a fun cookie to brag about. I like to add extra chocolate chips and sprinkles on top, which really makes it one-of-a-kind, and no one will know that it's not fully homemade!

Yield: 2 colossal cookies

1 (17.5-oz [490-g]) bag chocolate chip cookie mix
1 (17.5-oz [490-g]) bag sugar cookie mix
10 tbsp (120 g) rainbow sprinkles
½ cup (85 g) chocolate chips

Make the chocolate chip and sugar cookies according to package directions.

To assemble the cookies, line a jelly roll pan with parchment paper and use this as your work area.

Divide the chocolate chip cookie dough into 4 equal pieces. Roll each piece into a ball, and then use the palms of your hands to flatten it into a circle 4 inches (10 cm) in diameter.

Roll ¼ cup (60 g) of sugar cookie dough into a ball, and then use the palms of your hands to flatten it into a circle 2½ inches (6 cm) in diameter. Repeat to make a second circle. Set the flattened sugar cookie circles in the centers of 2 of the chocolate chip cookie circles. Use your fingers to press into the sugar cookie dough area to create a concave area for the sprinkles. Scoop 2 tablespoons (24 g) of sprinkles into the concave area of each cookie. Top with the other chocolate chip cookie dough. Use your fingers to pinch together the top and bottom edges of the chocolate chip cookie, and then smooth out the sides for a seamless colossal cookie.

Sprinkle the remaining rainbow sprinkles over the cookies, and use your fingers to press them in place on the top and sides. Spread the chocolate chips over the tops of the cookies and press them in place.

Place the tray of decorated cookies in the freezer for at least 15 minutes and preheat the oven to 350°F (177°C).

Bake one cookie at a time for 24 to 28 minutes, or until the edges are golden-brown. Once out of the oven, allow the cookie to cool down on the baking tray for about 15 minutes before moving it to the cooling rack, otherwise it could break apart easily if moved too soon.

Birthday Sprinkles Sugar Cookie

Everyone loves sprinkles! This cookie is bright, rainbow-colored and screams, "Play with me!" The sugar cookie mix easily lends itself to a birthday cake cookie! Just a touch of almond extract and rainbow sprinkles and there you have it! So simple and easy there are really no excuses not to try this one.

Yield: 2 colossal cookies

1 (17.5-oz [490-g]) bag sugar cookie mix

⅓ cup + 6 tbsp (136 g) rainbow sprinkles, divided

⅛ tsp almond extract

For the birthday cake cookie, whisk the sugar cookie mix with ⅓ cup (64 g) of rainbow sprinkles before following the packaging instructions. Prepare the mix as directed, adding the almond extract after the egg. Mix until the cookie dough just comes together and now the cookie is ready to be decorated!

To assemble the cookies, line a jelly roll pan with parchment paper and use this as your work area.

Divide the cookie dough in half evenly. Roll each piece into a ball, and use the palms of your hands to flatten it into a circle 5 inches (13 cm) in diameter.

Cover the cookies with the remaining rainbow sprinkles and use your fingers to press them in place.

Place the decorated cookies in the freezer for at least 15 minutes and preheat the oven to 350°F (177°C).

Bake one cookie at a time in the oven for 22 to 26 minutes, or until the edges are light golden-brown. Once out of the oven, allow the cookie to cool down on the baking tray for about 15 minutes before moving the cookie to the cooling rack, otherwise it could break apart easily if moved too soon.

Chocolate Chip + Espresso

If you love chocolate chip and chocolate, you'll find this double chocolate cookie combination just divine. Plus, the espresso powder added to the double chocolate chip will give anyone an extra boost of energy! I love having a cookie as an afternoon snack, and this one is ideal for getting me through those afternoons. If you're just having one of those days—this will turn your day right side up!

Yield: 2 colossal cookies

1 (17.5-oz [490-g]) bag chocolate chip cookie mix

1 (17.5-oz [490-g]) bag double chocolate chip cookie mix

1 tsp espresso powder

⅔ cup (113 g) chocolate chips

Follow the package instructions to make the chocolate chip cookie dough.

For the double chocolate chip cookie, whisk the cookie mix with the espresso powder, and then follow the package instructions to make the dough.

To assemble the cookies, line a jelly roll pan with parchment paper and use this as your work area.

Divide the chocolate chip cookie dough into 4 pieces. Roll each piece into a ball, and then use the palms of your hands to flatten it into a circle 4 inches (10 cm) in diameter.

Roll ¼ cup (60 g) of espresso double chocolate chip dough into a ball, and then use the palms of your hands to flatten it into a circle 2½ inches (6 cm) in diameter. Repeat to make a second espresso circle. Set the flattened espresso circles in the centers of 2 of the chocolate chip cookie circles. Top with the other chocolate chip circles. Use your fingers to pinch together the top and bottom edges of the cookie and smooth out the sides for a seamless colossal cookie.

Spread chocolate chips all over each cookie and gently press them onto the cookie dough to set them in place.

Place the tray of cookies in the freezer for at least 15 minutes and preheat the oven to 350°F (177°C).

Bake one cookie at a time in the oven for 24 to 28 minutes, or until the edges are golden-brown. Once the cookie is removed from the oven, allow it to cool down on the baking tray for about 15 minutes before moving it to the cooling rack. If moved too soon the cookie might break apart.

Oatmeal Chocolate Chip + Strawberry Preserves

Who wouldn't want to begin their day with a breakfast cookie? With the oatmeal full of fiber and the strawberry adding vitamins, you're taking the right step forward for a perfect day! The center filled with strawberry preserves adds a light fruity sweetness that makes this cookie so delightful in every way. If strawberry isn't your favorite, substitute with a flavor you like.

Yield: 2 colossal cookies

1 (17.5-oz [490-g]) bag oatmeal chocolate chip cookie mix

5 tbsp (75 ml) strawberry preserves

½ cup (66 g) coarsely chopped mixed nuts

Follow the package instructions to make the oatmeal chocolate chip cookie.

If you only have oatmeal cookie mix, and would like to add chocolate chips, after adding the ingredients needed for the dough to come together, stir in ¾ cup (128 g) of chocolate chips. If you prefer to go without chocolate chips, this will be just as delicious!

To assemble the cookies, line a jelly roll pan with parchment paper and use this as your work area.

Divide the oatmeal chocolate chip cookie dough into 4 pieces. Roll each piece into a ball, and then use the palms of your hands to flatten it into a circle 4 inches (10 cm) in diameter.

Use your fingers to gently press in the centers of 2 of the cookie circles to create a concave area to hold the preserves. Scoop 2½ tablespoons (38 ml) of preserves into the concave centers. Place the other flattened circles over the preserves. To prevent leaking, be careful not to press down onto the area with preserves. Use your fingers to pinch together the top and bottom edges of the cookies and smooth out the sides for a seamless colossal cookie.

Divide the nuts between the cookies and gently press them into the dough to set them in place.

Place the tray of cookies in the freezer for at least 15 minutes for the dough to set and preheat the oven to 350°F (177°C).

Bake one cookie at a time in the oven for 24 to 28 minutes, or until the edges are golden-brown. Allow the cookie to cool down on the baking tray for about 15 minutes. If moved too soon the cookie could break apart.

Oatmeal Cinnamon Chocolate Chip Trail Mix Cookie

This is one of my favorite breakfast cookies, and I try to defend in every way possible that it is a healthy start to the day! There are so many healthy components to this breakfast cookie—the oatmeal packed with fiber, cinnamon high in antioxidants and the nuts and peanut butter with protein, vitamins and omega-3 fatty acids. The heavenly combination of cinnamon with oatmeal complements the nut-filled trail mix, gooey peanut butter and slightly sweet chocolate chips. Do I really need to say much more?

If you would like, you could substitute your favorite chocolate spread for the peanut butter.

Yield: 2 colossal cookies

1 (17.5-oz [490-g]) bag oatmeal chocolate chip cookie mix
½ tsp ground cinnamon
½ cup (66 g) trail mix
6 tbsp (90 ml) peanut butter
½ cup (72 g) coarsely chopped trail mix

Whisk together the cookie mix and the ground cinnamon. Follow the package instructions to make the dough, and then fold the trail mix into the cookie dough.

If you only have oatmeal cookie mix, and would like to add chocolate chips, stir in ¾ cup (128 g) of chocolate chips after making the dough. If you prefer to go without chocolate chips, this will be just as delicious!

To assemble the cookies, line a jelly roll pan with parchment paper and use this as your work area.

Divide the cookie dough into 4 equal pieces. Roll each piece into a ball, and then use the palms of your hands to flatten each ball into a circle 4 inches (10 cm) in diameter.

Use your fingers to gently press in the centers of 2 of the circles to create a concave area to hold the peanut butter. Divide the peanut butter between the centers. Place the other oatmeal chocolate chip cookie circles over the peanut butter. Be careful not to press down onto the center area where the peanut butter is, or you'll find peanut butter oozing out from the sides. Use your fingers to pinch together the top and bottom edges of the cookie, and then smooth out the sides for a seamless colossal cookie.

Cover the tops of the cookies with chopped trail mix, and gently press it into the dough to set in place.

Place the tray of cookies in the freezer for at least 20 minutes and preheat the oven to 350°F (177°C).

Bake one cookie at a time for 24 to 28 minutes, or until the edges are golden-brown. Allow the cookie to cool down on the baking tray for about 15 minutes before moving the cookie to the cooling rack. If moved too soon the cookie could break apart.

Oatmeal Cinnamon Chocolate Chunk + Butterscotch

The creamy butterscotch pudding stuffed into this oatmeal cinnamon chocolate chunk cookie is what dreams are made of. The butterscotch flavor adds a light caramel touch to the overall cookie, and the pudding adds a smooth richness that creates the quintessential combination. The chocolate chunks add a deeper chocolatey flavor, and though it's still great with chocolate chips, it's just not quite right without the chunks on top. Take one bite and you'll know exactly what I mean.

Yield: 2 colossal cookies

¼ cup (13 g) butterscotch instant pudding mix

1 cup (240 ml) heavy cream

1 (17.5-oz [490-g]) bag oatmeal chocolate chip cookie mix

½ tsp ground cinnamon

⅔ cup (160 g) chocolate chunks

Make the butterscotch pudding so it has time to chill and set in the refrigerator. Whisk together the pudding mix and cream. The heavy cream is necessary to give the pudding the perfect velvety thickness for the cookie center. Once the pudding has come together and is fairly thick, place it in the refrigerator.

Whisk together the oatmeal chocolate chip cookie mix with the cinnamon. Then follow the package instructions to make the cookie dough.

If you only have oatmeal cookie mix, and would like to add chocolate chips, after adding the ingredients needed for the dough to come together, stir in ¾ cup (128 g) of chocolate chips. If you prefer to go without chocolate chips, this will be just as delicious!

To assemble the cookies, line a jelly roll pan with parchment paper and use this as your work area.

Divide the cookie dough into 4 equal pieces. Roll each piece into a ball, and then use the palms of your hands to flatten each ball into a circle 4 inches (10 cm) in diameter. Use your fingers to gently press in the centers of 2 of the circles to create slightly concave areas to hold the pudding.

Scoop 3 tablespoons (45 ml) of butterscotch pudding into both the centers. Place the other cookie dough circle over the pudding. Use your fingers to pinch together the top and bottom edges of the cookie, and then smooth out the sides for a seamless colossal cookie.

Spread chocolate chunks all over each cookie, and press gently to set them in place.

Place the tray of cookies in the freezer for at least 20 minutes for the cookie dough to set. Preheat the oven to 350°F (177°C).

Bake one cookie at a time for 24 to 28 minutes, or until the edges are golden-brown. Allow the cookie to cool down on the baking tray for about 15 minutes before moving it to the cooling rack. If moved too soon the cookie could break apart.

Peanut Butter Stuffed with Marshmallow

This is a fun version of the fluffernutter—a peanut butter sandwich with marshmallow fluff—but in cookie form. This colossal cookie will have everyone wanting more! The sweet, gooey marshmallow center is sandwiched by a slightly crisp peanut butter cookie exterior. The textures create the perfect contrast in every bite!

Yield: 2 colossal cookies

1 (17.5-oz [490-g]) bag peanut butter cookie mix

⅔ cup (30 g) of mini marshmallows or ½ cup (120 ml) of marshmallow fluff

Make the peanut butter cookie dough following the package directions.

To assemble the cookies, line a jelly roll pan with parchment paper and use this as your work area.

Divide the cookie dough into 4 equal pieces. Roll each piece into a ball, and then use the palms of your hands to flatten each ball into a circle 4 inches (10 cm) in diameter. Use your fingers to gently press in the centers of 2 of the circles to create a concave area to hold the marshmallow. Divide the marshmallows between the 2 circles. If you're using mini marshmallows, press the marshmallows together and gather them in the center of the cookie. For the marshmallow fluff, scoop the fluff into the concave center. Place the other flattened circle over the marshmallow. Use your fingers to pinch together the top and bottom edges of the cookie and smooth out the sides for a seamless cookie.

For the finishing touches, use either a chopstick or skewer and gently press it into the top of the cookie to create a grid pattern.

Place the tray with the cookies in the freezer for at least 20 minutes. Preheat the oven to 350°F (177°C).

Bake one cookie at a time for 24 to 28 minutes, or until the edges are golden-brown. Allow the cookie to cool down on the baking tray for about 15 minutes before moving the cookie to the cooling rack. If moved too soon the cookie could break apart.

Hot Chocolate–Chocolate Chip

I could always use a cup of hot chocolate on a winter day. But then there are those occasional chilly fall days when a hot chocolate would be welcomed, but it's just not cold enough for one. That's when I love baking a Hot Chocolate–Chocolate Chip cookie! And, don't you just hate it when you have a few sips of hot chocolate and all the marshmallows are gone? Well, if you're a marshmallow lover like me, you'll love that this cookie has a marshmallow center and fluffy and delicious marshmallow in every bite.

Yield: 2 colossal cookies

1 (17.5-oz [490-g]) bag chocolate chip cookie mix

¼ cup + 1 tbsp (42 g) instant hot chocolate mix (about 2 packets)

1 cup (45 g) mini marshmallows

½ cup (120 g) chocolate chunks

Whisk together the chocolate chip cookie mix with the hot chocolate. Then follow the package directions for making the cookie dough.

To assemble the cookies, line a jelly roll pan with parchment paper and use this as your work area.

Divide the cookie dough into 4 equal pieces. Roll each piece into a ball, and then use the palms of your hands to flatten each ball into a circle 4 inches (10 cm) in diameter. Use your fingers to gently press in the centers of 2 of the cookie circles to create a slight concave area to hold the mini marshmallows. Place ¼ cup (12 g) of the marshmallows on each circle. Place the other flattened hot chocolate-chocolate chip cookie dough over the marshmallows. Use your fingers to pinch together the top and bottom edges of the cookie and smooth out the sides for a seamless colossal cookie.

Gently press the remaining marshmallows and the chocolate chunks onto the cookies.

Place the tray with the cookies in the freezer for at least 20 minutes for the cookie dough to rest. Preheat the oven to 350°F (177°C).

Bake one cookie at a time for 24 to 28 minutes. Allow the cookie to cool down on the baking tray for about 15 minutes before moving it to the cooling rack. If moved too soon the cookie could break apart.

Chocolate Chip Stuffed with Cookies 'n' Cream

This recipe would be the absolute perfect one to make for a dinner party. Because, to put it simply, everyone will be talking about how fantastic and incredible your colossal cookies are. Once baked, this chocolate chip cookie will be about 9 inches (23 cm) in diameter! But, not only will you have this amazing colossal chocolate chip cookie stuffed with a cookies 'n' cream cookie, but to use up the remaining dough you can make a to-die-for cookies 'n' cream colossal cookie with marshmallow filling. Good luck fending off your flocking fans.

Yield: 1 colossal cookie

16 oz (454 g) refrigerated chocolate chip cookie dough

16 oz (454 g) refrigerated cookies 'n' cream cookie dough

⅓ cup (57 g) chocolate chips

2 Oreo cookies, crushed

To assemble the cookies, line a jelly roll pan with parchment paper and use this as your work area.

For the chocolate chip colossal cookie, split the chocolate chip cookie dough in half. Roll each half into a ball, and then use the palms of your hands to flatten each ball into a circle 5½ inches (14 cm) in diameter. Roll ½ cup (120 g) of cookies 'n' cream cookie dough into a ball, and then flatten it into a circle 4 inches (10 cm) in diameter. Place the cookies 'n' cream circle in the center of one of the flattened chocolate chip circles and top with the other chocolate chip circle. Use your fingers to pinch together the top and bottom edges of the colossal cookie, and then smooth out the sides to create a seamless finish. Top the cookie with chocolate chips and gently press them into the dough to set in place.

Sprinkle the Oreos on top of the cookie. Use your hands to gently press the crushed Oreos onto the cookie to help them set in place.

Place the tray with the cookie in the freezer for at least 20 minutes. Preheat the oven to 350°F (177°C).

Bake for 30 to 35 minutes, or until the edges are golden-brown. After the cookie is baked, allow it to cool down for about 20 minutes on the baking tray prior to moving it to the cooling rack. The colossal chocolate chip cookie is more fragile due to its size, and if moved too soon, it could easily break.

COOKIES 'N' CREAM STUFFED WITH MARSHMALLOW VARIATION:

All you need for this variation is the remaining cookies 'n' cream cookie dough and ¼ cup (12 g) of mini marshmallows. Split the dough evenly in half and roll each half into a ball. Use the palms of your hands to flatten each ball into a circle 4½ inches (11 cm) in diameter.

Place ¼ cup (12 g) of mini marshmallows in the center of one of the flattened circles. Since the marshmallows are fluffy and don't always stay put, try squeezing them together so they stick and hold together just long enough for you to seal them in. Place the other flattened circle over the mini marshmallows. Use your fingers to pinch together the top and bottom edges of the cookie, and then smooth out the sides to create a seamless finish.

Place the tray with the cookie in the freezer for at least 20 minutes. Preheat the oven to 350°F (177°C). Bake for 20 to 24 minutes or until the edges are light-brown and allow the cookie to rest on the baking tray before moving it to the cooling rack.

Chocolate Chip Walnut with Chocolate-Hazelnut Spread

The mixture of walnuts, mixed nuts and chocolate-hazelnut spread in this cookie creates a perfect balance of chocolate chip cookie and nutty goodness. This cookie is a winner all the way, and it'll be tough not to finish one whole cookie on your own—I know that was a challenge for me. I'm not sure how I lived without this cookie, but I for sure cannot live without it now!

If you can't find chocolate chip cookie dough with walnuts, chop ½ cup (59 g) of walnuts and fold them into the cookie dough. Continue to fold and re-fold the cookie dough until the walnuts appear to be evenly distributed.

Yield: 2 colossal cookies

16 oz (454 g) refrigerated chocolate chip walnut cookie dough

6 tbsp (90 ml) chocolate-hazelnut spread (I prefer Nutella)

½ cup (66 g) coarsely chopped mixed nuts

½ cup (85 g) chocolate chips

To assemble the cookies, line a jelly roll pan with parchment paper and use this as your work area.

Divide the chocolate chip walnut cookie dough into 4 equal pieces. Roll each piece into a ball, and then use the palms of your hands to flatten the balls into circles 4 inches (10 cm) in diameter.

Divide the chocolate-hazelnut spread between 2 of the flattened circles and spread around the centers. Take another flattened cookie dough circle and place it on top over the spread. Use your fingers to pinch together the top and bottom edges of the cookie, and then smooth out the sides for a seamless cookie.

Cover the cookies with nuts and chocolate chips and gently press them onto the dough to set them in place. Place the tray with the cookies in the freezer for at least 20 minutes for the dough to rest. Preheat the oven to 350°F (177°C).

Bake one cookie at a time for 20 to 24 minutes, or until the edges are golden-brown. Allow the cookie to cool down on the baking tray for about 15 minutes prior to moving it to the cooling rack. If moved too soon the cookie could break apart.

Chocolate Chip + Cookies 'n' Cream

Have you ever tried a chocolate chip cookie with Oreos? If not, it's a must and absolutely amazing! I love this combination for some of my most indulgent desserts and especially as an ice cream topping! The soft chocolate chip cookie is a great contrast to the crispy crushed Oreos on the inside. Truly a mouthful of fun!

Yield: 2 colossal cookies

16 oz (454 g) refrigerated chocolate chip cookie dough

6 Oreos, crushed

⅔ cup (113 g) chocolate chips

To assemble the cookies, line a jelly roll pan with parchment paper and use this as your work area.

Divide the chocolate chip cookie dough into 4 equal pieces. Roll each piece into a ball, and then use the palms of your hands to flatten the balls into circles 4 inches (10 cm) in diameter.

Crush 3 Oreos and place them in the center of one of the flattened cookie circles. Place another flattened cookie circle on top of the crushed Oreos. Use your fingers to pinch together the top and bottom edges of the cookie, and then smooth out the sides for a seamless cookie. Repeat for the second colossal cookie.

Spread the chocolate chips all over each cookie and gently press them onto the dough to set them in place. Place the tray with the cookies in the freezer for at least 20 minutes for the cookies to set. Preheat the oven to 350°F (177°C).

Bake one cookie at a time for 20 to 24 minutes, or until the edges are golden-brown. Allow the cookie to cool down for 15 minutes on the baking tray prior to moving it to the cooling rack. If moved too soon the cookie could break apart.

Oatmeal Raisin + Peanut Butter

Oatmeal combined with anything makes for one of the best breakfast cookies, but when combined with raisins and peanut butter it's especially good. This cookie isn't just for breakfast—it also makes a great afternoon snack. Imagine yourself and this cookie with your morning or afternoon coffee or tea! Life's too short to not treat yourself right, so go now and indulge!

Yield: 2 colossal cookies

16 oz (454 g) refrigerated oatmeal raisin cookie dough

6 tbsp (90 ml) peanut butter

⅔ cup (88 g) coarsely chopped mixed nuts

To assemble the cookies, line a jelly roll pan with parchment paper and use this as your work area.

Divide the oatmeal raisin cookie dough into 4 equal pieces. Roll each piece into a ball, and then use the palms of your hands to flatten the balls into circles 4 inches (10 cm) in diameter.

Divide the peanut butter between 2 of the cookie circles. Place the other cookie circles on top of the peanut butter. Use your fingers to pinch together the top and bottom edges of the cookies, and then smooth out the sides for a seamless cookie.

Cover both cookies with nuts and gently press them onto the cookie dough to set them in place. Place the tray with the cookies in the freezer for at least 20 minutes for the dough to rest. Preheat the oven to 350°F (177°C).

Bake one cookie at a time for 20 to 24 minutes, or until the edges are golden-brown. Allow the cookie to cool down for 15 minutes on the baking tray prior to moving it to the cooling rack. If moved too soon the cookie could break apart.

Sprinkle Sugar Cookie + Vanilla Pudding

This cookie is beautiful inside and out, from the sprinkles on the outside to the soft pudding inside. Biting into this cookie reminds me of biting into a pillowy soft doughnut filled with cream! The texture of the sugar cookie is fluffy, and when combined with a creamy and velvety vanilla pudding it brings me to a happy place. I'm pretty sure this euphoric state of mind doesn't happen very often. Enjoy it while it lasts!

Yield: 2 colossal cookies

¼ cup (13 g) vanilla instant pudding mix

1 cup (240 ml) heavy cream

16 oz (454 g) refrigerated sugar cookie dough

½ cup (96 g) sprinkles

Make the pudding by whisking together the pudding mix with the cream. After about 2 minutes, the mixture will thicken to a custard texture, which is exactly what we need for the filling. Place the pudding in the refrigerator to chill.

To assemble the cookies, line a jelly roll pan with parchment paper and use this as your work area.

Divide the sugar cookie dough into 4 equal pieces. Roll each piece into a ball, and then use the palms of your hands to flatten the balls into circles 4 inches (10 cm) in diameter. Use your fingers to gently press in the centers of 2 of the circles to create slightly concave areas to hold the pudding.

Place 3 tablespoons (45 ml) of pudding in each of the centers of 2 of the flattened circles. Take the other flattened cookie circles and place over the pudding. Use your fingers to pinch together the top and bottom edges of the cookies, and then smooth out the sides for a seamless cookie.

Cover the tops of both cookies with sprinkles and gently press them into the cookie dough to set them in place. Place the tray with the cookies in the freezer for at least 20 minutes for the cookie dough to rest. Preheat the oven to 350°F (177°C).

Bake one cookie at a time for 20 to 24 minutes, or until the edges are golden-brown. Allow the cookie to cool down for 15 minutes on the baking tray prior to moving it to the cooling rack. If moved too soon the cookie could break apart.

Just a Few Essentials

A stuffed cookie wouldn't be a stuffed cookie without some stuffing! Here are the essential recipes you need to step up your game. While there is always the store-bought route, the homemade version is just going to be that much better. If you have 5 to 20 minutes to spare, why not have homemade caramel or ganache incorporated into your amazing colossal cookie?

Salted Caramel

Salted caramel is one of my absolute favorite ingredients to use in a cookie, as a topping on a dessert and really, to just eat it on its own. It's so great that I always have a jar on hand at home—you know, just in case of an emergency. Though I've had my fair share of burnt caramels in the past, nothing can beat homemade. I've tried various ways of making caramel and found this to be one of the easiest ways, and I hope that you do too.

Yield: 1⅓ cups (320 ml)

1 cup (200 g) granulated white sugar

¼ cup (60 ml) light corn syrup

7 tbsp (98 g) unsalted butter, cubed and at room temperature

½ cup (120 ml) heavy cream, at room temperature

1 tsp sea salt

Line an 8 × 8-inch (20 × 20-cm) pan with parchment paper. Use a wooden spoon or heatproof spatula to stir together the sugar and light corn syrup in a heavy saucepan on medium heat. If you have a candy thermometer, it is best to use it to avoid burning the caramel. Stir continuously while the sugar is cooking. The sugar will go through a few phases before turning into caramel. Keep a careful eye on the sugar as it can burn quickly, and it can go from 300°F to 350°F (149°C to 177°C) in a matter of seconds.

When the sugar temperature reaches 350°F (177°C), reduce the heat to low and slowly add in the butter. The butter may cause the sugar mixture to bubble, but continue to stir. As the butter melts, slowly add in the cream. The cream may cause the mixture to bubble again, and if the heavy cream is too cold, it may cause the caramel to harden, but continue to stir and it will turn into liquid again. One way to avoid the bubbling caused by the butter and heavy cream is to microwave them for about 20 to 30 seconds, but this is not a necessary step.

As the caramel is boiling, add in the sea salt. Continue to stir for another 20 minutes to boil off some of the liquid. Pour the salted caramel into the pan, and let it sit on the side to cool down for about 20 minutes, and then pour it into a heatproof container and allow it to cool down completely. Once it has reached room temperature, keep it in the refrigerator.

Salted caramel needs to cool down before being incorporated in any recipe, so be sure to allow plenty of time to chill.

Dark Chocolate Ganache

The quality of chocolate used in any recipe is always important. The fine notes within the chocolate will enhance your cookies, and therefore, using high quality chocolate to make your ganache is very important. It may sound easier to buy a jar from a store, but unless it is a reputable brand of chocolate ganache, which then means it could be pricy, it may not do your cookie any justice. Making ganache is so simple and takes less than 10 minutes from start to finish! This one is definitely worth the small effort.

Yield: ⅞ cup (207 ml)

½ cup (120 ml) heavy cream
⅔ cup (113 g) dark chocolate chips
Pinch of salt

Use a whisk to stir the cream and chips together in a heavy saucepan over medium heat. The chocolate chips will melt quickly and soon enough will be incorporated smoothly into the cream for a chocolate ganache!

Finish it by whisking in a pinch of salt. Pour the ganache into a heatproof container and set aside to completely cool down. Once cool, place the container in the refrigerator. Note that when the ganache is refrigerated, it will be harder to scoop, but it will make it easier to place and control for the cookie stuffing.

White Chocolate Ganache

If you've never made chocolate ganache before, you'll be surprised at how quick and easy it is. In less than 10 minutes—it should really take no more than 5—you'll have homemade ganache. It's so simple that there is no excuse not to try it out!

Yield: 1½ cups (360 ml)

½ cup (120 ml) heavy cream
2 cups (340 g) white chocolate chips
Pinch of salt

Use a whisk to stir the cream and chips together in a heavy saucepan over medium heat. The chips will melt quickly and will soon be incorporated smoothly into the cream for a white chocolate ganache!

Finish it by whisking in a pinch of salt. Pour the ganache into a heatproof container, and set aside to cool down completely. Once cool, place the container in the refrigerator. Note that if the ganache is refrigerated, it will be harder to scoop, but it will make it that much easier to place and control for the cookie stuffing.

Cheesecake

Have you ever had fluffy cheesecake? I don't just mean any kind of cheesecake, but an airy and soft cheesecake that is mouthwatering and delicious. If you haven't, you have to try this cheesecake recipe immediately! It's so simple that there are no excuses. Though the mixer has to mix the cream cheese for a number of minutes, it's the mixer doing the job, not you. So just sit back and relax, and watch the cheesecake batter grow in fluffiness as air is whipped into the mixture.

Yield: 1 (6-inch [15-cm]) cheesecake

8 oz (227 g) cream cheese, at room temperature

⅓ cup (67 g) granulated white sugar

1 large egg, at room temperature

1 tsp pure vanilla extract

It is important to have the cream cheese at room temperature to avoid having too many chunks while the mixer is blending. Any clumps will eventually go away, but it could take longer if there are too many.

Preheat the oven to 325°F (163°C). Line a 6-inch (15-cm) round or square pan with parchment paper and make sure there is some overhang over the edges of the pan. I prefer parchment paper because the overhanging paper makes it easier to pull the cheesecake out from the pan, but you do lose the smooth finish on the edges due to the ridges in the parchment paper. Since the cheesecake is for the stuffing in the cookie, it's okay that the edges aren't perfect.

Use the paddle attachment on a stand mixer to blend the cream cheese and sugar together on low speed. Once the mixture comes together after about 3 to 5 minutes, even if there are a few clumps, add in the egg and then the vanilla. Allow the mixer to continue on low speed until there are no longer any clumps, which can take up to 15 minutes. Once the batter is smooth and creamy, use a spatula to help scrape the cheesecake batter into the pan.

Bake the cheesecake for about 30 minutes and allow it to cool down by turning off the oven and leaving the oven door open slightly. You'll notice that the cheesecake rises up while baking. The best way to prevent it from sinking too much is to allow it to cool down slowly. You can remove the cheesecake immediately from the oven, but the cheesecake will deflate, which will be fine, because the cheesecake will be flattened once it's stuffed into the cookie. Since I personally love fluffy cheesecake and there will be leftovers, you will definitely find me indulging on fluffy cheesecake while the cookie is baking. Such a special treat for yourself after baking!

Chocolate Brownie

A great brownie has an amazing chocolatey texture that is thick and chewy and just so delicious. The best part about this indulgent treat is how quick and easy it is to make. This is a great recipe that can be made the night before you use it to stuff your colossal cookies, but you'll just need to control yourself and hide it from others in your home so there is some left for stuffing!

Yield: 4 (4-inch [10-cm]) square brownies

½ cup (63 g) all-purpose flour

1 cup (200 g) granulated white sugar

¼ tsp salt

1 cup (227 g) unsalted butter

1 cup (86 g) cocoa powder

4 large eggs, at room temperature

1½ tsp (7 ml) pure vanilla extract

Preheat the oven to 325°F (177°C) and line an 8 × 8-inch (20 × 20-cm) pan with parchment paper. Make sure that there is extra parchment paper hanging over the edges of the pan so you can easily pull the brownies out from the pan.

Whisk together the flour, sugar and salt and set aside.

In a heavy saucepan, melt the butter on medium-low heat. Once the butter is melted, use a whisk to stir in the cocoa. After combining the butter and cocoa, use a spatula to scrape the mixture into a heatproof bowl. You can use a mixer for the next part, but be sure not to overmix.

Allow the butter mixture to cool for a few minutes and then whisk in one egg at a time. Fully incorporate each egg before proceeding. The mixture should come together with a thick, smooth texture. Whisk in the vanilla. Incorporate the flour mixture and stir until just combined.

Pour the brownie batter into the prepared pan and bake for 35 to 45 minutes. After the brownie is out of the oven and has cooled for a few minutes, pull it out by the overhanging parchment paper and rest the brownie on a cooling rack until cool.

Toffee

The next best thing after caramel is toffee! It has the nutty and buttery flavor that is similar to caramel, but it's crispy! The ingredients are similar to caramel minus the heavy cream. Also, it's so much easier to make compared to caramel. So simple to make, plus it's delicious—there's definitely no excuse to not go homemade on this one.

Yield: 1⅜ cups (214 g)

½ cup (114 g) unsalted butter
½ cup (100 g) granulated white sugar
⅛ tsp salt

Line a jelly roll pan with parchment paper or aluminum foil.

On medium heat, use either a wooden spoon or a heatproof spatula to stir together the butter and sugar in a heavy sauce pan. A candy thermometer is useful, but not necessary since toffee is fairly easy to make. The butter and sugar mixture will bubble as it is cooking and eventually turn to an amber color at 250°F (121°C), which is when you should remove the pan from the heat. Continue to mix and add in the salt. Be careful at this point, as you can burn yourself with the toffee.

Spread the liquid toffee over the parchment paper and let it set. After about 10 to 15 minutes, place the tray into the refrigerator or freezer for the toffee to crisp. Once the toffee has hardened, use a knife to chop the toffee into smaller pieces. You will have extra toffee left over after making the cookie, so definitely don't hold back from snacking on some while you're baking!

Vanilla Buttercream

This luscious vanilla buttercream is fluffy and tastes light as air. It's incredibly smooth and will definitely have you wanting more. I love this buttercream for many desserts, and it's my go-to for cupcakes! Though the mixing process sounds time-consuming, all you need to do is turn on the mixer to the required speed and set a timer. Before you know it, you'll have light-as-a-cloud buttercream that you'll be making time and time again.

Yield: 1½ cups (360 ml)

½ cup (114 g) unsalted butter, at room temperature

1 cup plus 2 tbsp (113 g) sifted powdered sugar

1 tsp pure vanilla extract

1½ tbsp (22 ml) heavy cream or heavy whipping cream

Pinch of salt

Use the paddle attachment to cream together the butter and sugar for 6 minutes on medium speed. The mixture will be very fluffy and almost white in color. Reduce the mixer speed to low, and add in the vanilla and the cream. Keep the mixer on low speed until those ingredients are well combined, and then add in a pinch of salt. Increase the mixer speed back to medium and allow it to continue for another 5 minutes. Finally, your amazingly soft and silky buttercream is ready!

Lemon Curd

I love lemon curd stuffed in cookies, but I also love it in a lemon meringue tart or pie. The sweet and tart flavor is addictive; plus the beautiful bright color and the smooth texture make it so perfect. Another plus is how surprisingly easy lemon curd is to make. This is one of those things that everyone thinks is very complicated and fancy, but really it takes less than 15 minutes to make. So, actually—don't tell your friends about how easy this is. Show it off and let them ooh and aah over it.

Yield: 1 cup (240 ml)

¾ tbsp (11 g) lemon zest, approximately 2–3 lemons

½ cup (120 ml) fresh lemon juice, approximately 2–3 lemons

½ cup plus 1 tbsp (113 g) granulated white sugar

3 large eggs, at room temperature

5 tbsp (70 g) unsalted butter, at room temperature

Pinch of salt

If you are hand juicing the lemons, don't worry if the pulp gets mixed in because we will be straining the lemon curd at the end.

In a heavy saucepan, whisk together the lemon zest, lemon juice, sugar and eggs on low heat. Continue to whisk as the mixture comes together and begins to thicken. Sometimes the egg will cook a little bit, and you may see egg white strands, but this is okay since we will strain out the curd in the end. Once the mixture has thickened, add in the butter and pinch of salt. Feel free to taste, and if you would like it a little sweeter add a teaspoon of additional sugar. Once the mixture has thickened or reached 170°F (77°C), remove the saucepan from the heat.

Place a fine mesh strainer over a medium bowl and use a spatula to scrape the lemon curd into the strainer. Since the lemon curd may not go through the strainer easily, use the spatula to gently push the lemon curd through. Any lemon pulp or egg white strands will be left behind in the strainer, leaving you with a beautiful golden-yellow curd.

Allow the lemon curd to cool completely before placing it in a container. Refrigerate until needed.

Browned Butter

Browned butter adds an element of nutty deliciousness to any cookie. When butter is cooked, the bits of milk protein in the butter begin to brown and release an amazing nutty aroma. When you use browned butter in a cookie, that nutty flavor gets infused into the cookie. Also, though a recipe may not call for browned butter, I've found that browned butter can easily be incorporated into most cookie recipes.

Butter, as needed

To brown the butter, place any amount of unsalted butter needed for a recipe or yield in a heavy saucepan over medium-low heat and stir the butter occasionally. The cream-colored milk protein deposits will begin to separate from the butter and will slowly brown.

After about 6 minutes, the butter will start to bubble. This is when it's crucial to keep an eye on the butter, because once the butter begins to brown, it can burn easily. It should take about 8 to 10 minutes to brown the butter. After the butter is browned, pour it into a bowl.

Roasted Bananas

When you roast a banana, it brings out a caramelized flavor that makes the banana that much sweeter. If you're a fan of bananas, like me, then definitely consider substituting roasted bananas for mashed bananas in any recipe.

Yield: 1 cup (85 g)

3-4 ripe bananas

Preheat the oven to 400°F (204°C). Line a jelly roll pan with aluminum foil, fold up the edges and pinch together the corners. This step makes for easy cleanup because as the bananas are roasting the juices will leak out and tend to stick to the pan.

Use a knife to cut a 4-inch (10-cm) long slit down the side of the bananas. Do not cut all the way through the banana. Bake for 20 minutes. The bananas will start to sizzle. Remove the bananas from the oven and allow them to cool down for 5 to 10 minutes. Once cooled down a bit, peel the bananas and allow the juice to drain out before mashing.

Techniques and Tips

Though not the most exciting, it is necessary to make a few points on key aspects of colossal cookies to ensure that each and every cookie turns out as perfect as possible. After all, baking can be a little daunting, so I hope that with the tips below you will have a fabulous colossal cookie every time!

MEASUREMENTS

The most accurate way to measure for baking is to use a scale. Since not everyone has one, we use cups, teaspoons and tablespoons. However, one scooped cup of all-purpose flour by one person is not always the same as one scooped by another person. So what happens after all the ingredients are incorporated and the cookie dough ends up being a little on the dry side? If I find the dough to be a little dry, one of my secrets balancing it all out without altering the taste is to add 1 tablespoon (15 ml) of heavy cream at a time to the cookie dough in the mixer until the cookie dough is moist, but not sticky. If this were ever needed, I would say a maximum of 3 tablespoons (45 ml) would be the most anyone should ever add.

CREAMING THE BUTTER AND SUGAR

Generally in the directions I indicate that the butter and sugar are to be creamed together for 2 to 3 minutes. This step is essential, so I will underline its importance here. When the paddle to the mixer is whipping the butter and sugar together, it is whipping air into the mixture, which is why the creamed butter and sugar becomes fluffy in texture and light and pale in color. The air in the mixture gives your cookies the lightness to make them amazingly delicious.

SEALING A STUFFED COOKIE

I can't stress this enough for getting a fantastic outcome with a stuffed cookie. This is so important, especially when contents such as caramel and chocolate can turn liquid when they are baking, or marshmallow stuffing can expand while baking. When the top and bottom cookie circles are pinched together, it creates a seal, but there is still a seam that can easily open while the cookie is baking. Therefore, after pinching together the top and bottom edges, the edges need to be smoothed out so the seams are no longer visible to create a more secure seal around the ingredients stuffed inside.

BAKING

A fully preheated oven is extremely important. I recommend an oven thermometer to ensure that the oven is at the correct temperature.

I always recommend baking on either a silicone baking mat or parchment paper, rather than directly on the baking tray.

The baking time provided is a range. Begin checking for doneness at the least amount of bake time. The colossal cookie should be dome-shaped prior to baking. One key way to know that it is ready to be taken out of the oven is when the cookie has flattened out. If there is still a slight dome shape to the cookie or the top center looks as though it is raw dough and does not have a crisp appearance, add another 3 to 5 minutes and check back on the cookie.

In most cases, the cookie will be around 4 to 5 inches (10 to 12 cm) in diameter prior to baking and will spread out to 6 to 8 inches (15 to 20 cm) once baked. So unless you have a larger than ordinary oven, definitely bake one cookie at a time for the best results.

Pay attention to the sides of the cookie. If there are slight cracks, this is another sign that the cookie could be done, but this should be the last of the indicators used to determine if the cookie is fully baked.

When moving the cookie to the cooling rack, I recommend sliding the parchment paper or silicone baking mat onto the cooling rack with the cookie on it. These cookies are very delicate when warm. When the cookie is cooling down, it is still baking on the inside, so be sure to handle the cookie with care.

Definitely feel free to freeze the unbaked cookies for up to a week or two. If you do not intend on baking right away, wrap each cookie in plastic wrap to protect it from potential freezer burn. You want the dough to be kept fresh for a fantastic cookie once you are ready to bake it! No thaw time is needed; you can place the cookie straight from the freezer into the oven.

Acknowledgments

First and foremost, I have to thank all my readers. You are the foundation of My Dessert Diet. You have been encouraging, supportive and, most importantly, loyal, continuing to return to see what I love to do. I love you and would not be here doing what I love without your dedicated love for colossal cookies. So, thank you from the bottom of my heart, and I can't wait for you to try out all these recipes. You can make your own colossal cookies and share them with your friends and family!

In addition to my fans, I would like to endlessly thank Page Street Publishing for discovering me and taking a chance on a first-time author, who is in retail merchandising by day and blogging by night. This would not be possible without you, I am 1,000 percent forever grateful for this opportunity and believing in me and making a girl's dream come true.

Next, I have to thank my wonderful husband for his patience, because our less than 500 square foot Brooklyn apartment was turned into a test kitchen. We had various ingredients—flour, white sugar, light brown sugar, dark brown sugar, sprinkles—you name it, we had it in our apartment somewhere, covering our floors or on a desk or chair. My cookie testing was found everywhere, along with baking trays and piles of cookies covering every surface imaginable. Basically, we lived among cookies, and he was overruled by them. I also need to thank my husband because I am not a cook, I am a baker, and he is actually the cook in our home. The food that was cooked to keep us alive and to balance the cookie taste-testing was made by him, and he had to cook among cookies and baking supplies all over the place. Needless to say, he does have a weakness for cookies, so maybe he appreciated all this after all?

Of course, my parents, who have supported me along the way from my early childhood days and taught me how to bake. They have always loved my crazy imagination and creativity and have endlessly helped me flourish along the way. I've always come up with crazy stories, and they just embraced it all. I'm not sure what they ever thought I'd grow up doing, but maybe they just knew one day that I would be combining my talents into one. My love for baking and my crazy imagination together brought us to colossal cookies!

Lastly, my incredibly patient friends, who perhaps are actually super thankful that I was writing this book and needed taste-testers, who endured endless amounts of cookie combinations and taste-testing. I'm pretty sure that at one point they secretly wished that I wasn't going to find them, so they could get back on their diet plans. Lucky for me, I have an amazingly supportive group of friends who love what I do, appreciate me for me and really aren't always on a diet. So, cheers to them, who've probably gained the equivalent to a freshman 15 (or more), just for me and you.

About the Author

Wendy Kou grew up on the east coast and has been living in Brooklyn, New York for over 10 years. Though she's a luxury retail buyer by day, you can definitely count on her to be eating and baking away with every free moment.

Wendy has always loved food and baking and has been baking for as long as she can remember. She has taken inspiration from her mom, who has an incredible passion for baking. She's a self-taught baker, and she tested out various recipes from cookbooks and websites before she found her way to creating her very own recipes.

Wendy's love for food starts with sweets and desserts. She could start and end a meal with dessert, or just have dessert for a meal, hence the name of her blog My Dessert Diet. She started her blog on December 31, 2014 with a cookie post, and has since developed a number of various types of recipes, which she shares on the blog. Most importantly, Wendy always try to keep the blog special, by taking the ordinary to extraordinary!

Lastly, she enjoys sharing photos of her creations, favorite restaurants and travels on her Instagram @wendykou. Wendy can't wait for you to join her in her adventures! She would love to hear from you!

Index